10 MINUTE Kabbalah

10 MINUTE Kabbalah

Blessings, Wisdom, and Guidance from the Tree of Life

SHOSHANNA COHEN

FAIR WINDS
PRESS
GLOUCESTER, MASSACHUSETTS

First published in the USA in 2003 by
Fair Winds Press
33 Commercial Street
Gloucester, MA 01930

Library of Congress Cataloging-in-Publication Data available

ISBN 1-59233-027-4

10 9 8 7 6 5 4 3

Cover design by Laura Shaw Design
Cover Illustration by Elizabeth Cornaro
Book design by *tabula rasa* graphic design
Printed and bound in Canada

I dedicate this book to my aunt and uncle,
Gloria and Dick Raskin, who have shown
me the importance of honoring both
my family and my heritage.

CONTENTS

INTRODUCTION

The Time for Kabbalah Knowledge Is Now

When I was growing up in a reform Jewish home in the 1960s and '70s no one ever mentioned Kabbalah to me—not even in Hebrew school (two afternoons a week) or Sunday school (another two hours each week). In fact, I still remember the first time someone asked me about Kabbalah. I was in my early twenties, and I had to admit I didn't know anything about it. I somehow felt un-Jewish. The Christian woman who asked me the question knew something about my own religion and ancestry that I didn't know.

I don't remember who told me what Kabbalah was, but I do remember what I was told: Kabbalah was a mystical kind of Jewish study, something only very Orthodox Jews studied. And many more liberal Jews (in other words, more educated, secular Jews) thought it was a kind of "black magic."

So I wrote it off.

About ten years later, I went to graduate school to study Eastern philosophy and religion and, suddenly, everyone was talking about Kabbalah. And they took it seriously. I had to find out for myself what it was all about.

Now, at the beginning of the 21st century, as a woman in my early forties, I have brought my study of Kabbalah full circle. Kabbalah has enabled me to reconcile my Jewish ancestry—with its respect for intellectual curiosity and study—with my longing for a spiritual connection to the universe.

Like me, many other people, both Jews and non-Jews, have found that the religion of their childhood hasn't sustained them through adulthood, and yet they don't want to turn their backs on belief. They are trying to create a spiritual bond between themselves and their concept of God.

Of course, you may ask, why did I write what I hope will be a popular book on Kabbalah? Well, I became a little frustrated with my research, because a lot of books on Kabbalah seem to say very little while encouraging people to read more and more. And while it's true that Judaism asks it members to study as much as possible, it suddenly seemed too vague to me. I don't want to spend my life reading books, nor do I want to spend my life reading just one book. I was looking for a philosophy—an answer— that would encourage me to live my life and give me spiritual guidance on how to live it well.

But before I get into the details of what my study of the Kabbalah has given me, I'd like to tell you a little about Judaism. Although traditional Orthodox Jewish thinkers would disagree with me, as far as I'm concerned, it isn't necessary to be Jewish to understand and accept Kabbalah. However, Kabbalah was born from Judaism and to understand fully its creation and its study, you should at least have a basic knowledge of the Jewish religion.

What do Jews believe?

Once, during a time in my life when I felt alienated from my heritage, I asked my favorite uncle why he was Jewish. My uncle has one of the most rational and logical minds I've ever encountered, with two advanced degrees (economics and law). He's so rational and so logical that he's actually quite irritating to those of us who consider ourselves to be more on the emotional side. Anyway, I asked him once, why, with his rational mind, he was still such an observant Jew.

"Judaism," my uncle explained to me, "allows us to believe whatever works for us and still be Jewish. You don't even have to believe in God to be Jewish!"

Now, my uncle is definitely one of a kind, but the truth is, all sorts of people recognize their Jewish heritage but don't necessarily practice the traditions of Judaism that their grandparents and great-grandparents practiced. The beliefs and practices of Judaism range from Hasidic to Orthodox to Conservative to Reform to Reconstructionist—and each of these groups has its own understanding of the Jewish tenets.

It's important to know, too, that Judaism is not a race (you can be black and Jewish or Asian and Jewish or white and Jewish), nor is it a nationality (Jews live in various countries around the world). It is a religion—nothing more and nothing less—a belief system that explains the Divine and how we should exist in this world.

Below are thirteen principles of faith, written by Ramban, a Spanish scholar who lived in the early 13th century. He considered a belief in these ideas to be the minimum requirements of being a Jew.

- God exists.
- There is only one God. God is unique.
- God is incorporeal and has no physical body.

- God is eternal.
- You pray to God alone, with no intermediary, and you pray to no others.
- The words of the Prophets are true.
- Moses' prophecies are true and Moses was the greatest of the Prophets.
- God gave the Torah (the first five books of the Bible) and the Talmud (additional writings and commentary on the Torah) to Moses and they are true.
- There is and will be no other Torah.
- God knows the thoughts and deeds of all people.
- God will reward the good and punish the wicked.
- The Moschiach[1] will come.
- The dead will be resurrected.

---

[1] Jews try not to use the word "Messiah" because the Jewish concept of Messiah is very different from the Christian word. I will explain the difference between the two words shortly.

As you can see, these beliefs do not mention how to live your life (whether to keep a kosher home, for example) or how often you must attend synagogue. These tenets do not discuss how to dress; whom to date; or whether and how to observe any religious rituals and life events, such as circumcision, Bar and Bat Mitzvahs, marriage, and death. There is no mention about Israel or learning Hebrew.

That is not to say that Jews don't concern themselves with the kinds of rules that govern how to live our lives. In fact, according to Orthodox Judaism, God gave Moses six hundred and thirteen commandments (not simply ten; the Ten Commandments are just the real biggies). Those commandments include a very long list of laws and customs that Jews are also supposed to follow. The customs govern such things from how to wash in the morning to how to go to bed at night—and everything in between.

But this book is not concerned with leading a more observant Jewish life, i.e., following a long list of customs. Instead, I have taken the teaching of Kabbalah and used it as a way to bring an individual—any individual—closer to God. But, before we can understand how the Kabbalah will bring us closer to God, we first have to understand what Jews mean when they talk about God.

What is the Jewish concept of God?

Jews believe that God created the universe and that the actual existence of a universe is the only proof of God that we need. Jews recite the prayer, "Hear O Israel, the Lord is God, the Lord is One," and by that we mean, "Listen! There is just one God and you should pray to no other." This is significant because throughout history people have prayed to idols and saints. Jews do not do this. When they pray, they pray straight to God; they don't tell their prayers to an intermediary. It's not that prayers are secret, it's just that we don't believe one person has a closer link to God than the rest of us (which isn't to say that we don't recognize the knowledge and goodness of our rabbis, it's just that we don't believe God loves the smart ones better).

Although people use language that describes God as having physical attributes, such as "the Hand of God," Jews do not believe God has a body. These are just elements of poetic license. And actually, many Jews, especially those interested in Kabbalah, would argue that this type of speech (such as personification) makes the true vision of God fuzzy, changing Him from a spirit to a person.

So, why did I use the word "Him"? Since God has no body, Jews don't understand God to be a man, or a woman. We sometimes use the word "He" to discuss God because of the limits of language, but not for any other reason and, once again, this kind of shorthand can misrepresent what we believe God to be. In the end, when Jews say that people are made in the "image" of God, we are referring to the goodness and ability of God, not the physical attributes of people or the spirit.

One more thing: Because Jews believe that God is a spirit, more than a kind of "super person," we also do not believe that God is an old man who judges people based on the goodness of their actions or the lack of sin in their lives. We do not pray to God for forgiveness, exactly (I'll go into this further when we actually discuss the Kabbalah), or believe that by doing a certain thing (such as reciting the Hail Mary) we are cleansed of sin.

This, of course, brings me to the next big question:

Why don't Jews believe Jesus Christ is the Messiah?

Jewish people are not looking for, or waiting for, the Son of God, a man who will die for our sins, or a man who is the product of a virgin birth. The very things that make Jesus' story compelling to Christians are the same things that convince Jews that Jesus isn't the Moschiach.

The Talmud says, "There is no difference between this world and the Messianic Age, except with regard to our subjugation by other governments." In a Messiah, Jews are looking for a political and spiritual leader who is a very real person. In fact, Jews believe that the Moschiach can be anyone at anytime. The real deal will show up when the world is ready for him or her, not before and not after. The Moschiach has as much to do with the way humankind is behaving as it does with the anointment of one particular human being. The only way to tell whether someone really is the Moschiach is whether he or she accomplishes the mission. If he or she doesn't return the exiles, inspire us to follow the Torah, and rebuild the Temple, he or she is not the Moschiach, as it says, "He shall not fail nor be crushed until he has set right the world" (Isaiah 42:4).

At this point in time, not all Jews are waiting for the Moschiach. Although the messianic concept is listed above as one of the minimum requirements needed to be a Jew, I would amend it by saying that to be a Jew you don't have to be waiting for the Messiah, but you are pretty convinced he hasn't already been here.

For our purposes, it's just significant to know that the study of Kabbalah is not related in any way with the idea of a Messiah. The Kabbalah offers instructions on how to lead a more spiritual life and be more connected with God; it is not a text describing how to bring about a new age or how to recognize or become the Moschiach.

Does Kabbalah have anything to do with Israel?

Kabbalah and the State of Israel (or a person's opinion of Israel) have no inherent relationship. Kabbalah is a means of spiritual study, while the creation of the State of Israel is mostly a political distinction.

In the late 1800s, Theodor Herzl and Chaim Weizmann began a political (not a religious) movement called Zionism, which called for the creation of a Jewish state in Israel. But, even more than one hundred years ago, the idea of a Jewish state created exactly what we have today: both support for and hatred from various parties around the world. Even as early as the 20th century, Arabs, Jews, and Palestinians (who, when Zionism first started, weren't considered separate from other Arabs) argued over who got what land.

Immediately before and just after World War II, the idea of a Jewish homeland seemed to be more important than ever—Jews had a lot of trouble leaving Western Europe because few countries wanted to take them in, despite the threat (and reality) of genocide. At this point, the land that was then called Palestine was under British rule, but in 1947, the United Nations divided the land between the Jews and the Arabs for them to self-govern. In 1948, Jews created the State of Israel, which was officially recognized by several Western countries.

Surrounding Arab countries were not so quick to agree to the legitimacy of a Jewish state. In fact, the Arabs fought a yearlong war to drive out the Jews. Miraculously, the new state of Israel won the war, as well as every subsequent Arab-Israeli war, gaining territory each time the Arabs attacked them.

Today, approximately five million Jews, more than a third of the world's Jewish population, live in Israel. Jews make up more than eighty percent of the population of the land, and Jews are in political control of the country. Under Israel's Law of Return, any Jew who has not converted to another religion can automatically become an Israeli citizen.

Although there is a very small group of right-wing Jews, mostly Orthodox, who don't recognize the legitimacy of the State of Israel because the Moschiach has not yet come, most Jews today support the existence of the State of Israel, even those who might feel uncomfortable with some of the country's actions.

Why do some Jews seem more traditional than others?

Until almost two hundred years ago, there were only two kinds of Jews: the Ashkenazic Jews of Eastern Europe and the Sephardic Jews of Spain and the Middle East. Although each group lived in a different area of the world, they practiced similar styles of Judaism and believed in the same things. The biggest differences between them were the foods they ate and the clothes they wore. Ashkenazic Jews wore more clothing (lots of dark coats and fur hats) and ate lots of potato dishes (we can thank these ancestors for kugel, blintzes, and latkes) because they lived in cold climates. Sephardic Jews drank more wine and ate more fruit. Other than that, a Jew was a Jew was a Jew.

But, just as with the rest of the world and society, times have changed. There are thirteen million Jews in the world today (and yes, there were millions more before the Holocaust; we haven't brought our numbers back up to that level and most likely never will). About five million of them live in the United States.

Between the United States and Israel, there are four main Jewish denominations: Orthodox, Conservative, Reform, and Reconstructionist. Orthodox and sometimes Conservative are described as "traditional" movements. Reform, Reconstructionist, and sometimes Conservative are described as "liberal" or "modern" movements.

The Orthodox movements are very similar in belief. They all believe that God gave Moses the whole Torah at Mount Sinai. The "whole Torah" includes both the Written Torah (the first five books of the Bible) and the Oral Torah, an oral tradition interpreting and explaining the Written Torah. Orthodox Jews believe that the Torah is true, that it has come down to us intact and unchanged. They believe that the Torah contains six hundred and thirteen mitzvoth (good deeds) binding upon Jews.

About seven percent of the Jews in America identify themselves as Orthodox. Some of these Orthodox Jews are Hasidic, which means they organize around a spiritual leader called a rebbe (rabbi or teacher). A Hasid consults his rebbe about all major life decisions. Hasids continue to wear dark clothing and maintain other "old-fashioned" physical traditions; men don't cut their sideburns (*payas*) and women often wear wigs in front of everyone but their husbands.

Conservative Jews believe that the Torah comes from God, but they believe that the laws of Judaism were correct to change a bit over time and that a person can be a Jew while still adapting to the society in which he or she lives. There are fewer Conservative Jews than Reform Jews in the United States today, and each Conservative synagogue is different. Some are closer to Orthodox while others are closer to Reform.

Reform Jews are the most liberal bunch. Reforms Jews do not believe God wrote the Torah, but that it is a collection of writings by separate authors strung together over time. Reform Jews do not live by the laws of Judaism (many of them do not keep kosher homes and will marry outside of their faith), but they still consider themselves to be Jewish. Almost half of the Jews in the United States consider themselves Reform.

Technically, Reconstructionist Judaism grew out of the Conservative movement. Reconstructionists believe that Judaism is an "evolving religious civilization." They do not believe in a personified deity that is active in history, and they do not believe that God chose the Jewish people. From this, you might assume that Reconstructionism is to the left of Reform; yet Reconstructionism places much greater stress on Jewish observance than Reform Judaism does. Reconstructionists observe the traditional Jewish laws if they choose to, not because to do so is a binding Law from God but because it is a valuable part of our heritage—which many more-dominant cultures have sought to destroy over the years.

I've been to every kind of synagogue and basically, the differences among the ceremonies amount to the language used

(Orthodox and Conservative use much more Hebrew, and Orthodox often uses only Hebrew), the clothes worn (Reform Jews are more casual), and how long the service is (all day at the stricter synagogues). In Orthodox shuls (Yiddish for "synagogues"), men and women sit in separate areas.

Orthodox Judaism is the only denomination that is formally and legally recognized in Israel. Until very recently, only Orthodox Jews could serve on religious councils. The Orthodox rabbinate in Israel controls matters of personal status, such as marriage and divorce, and conversion. However, more than half of all Israelis describe themselves as secular. About fifteen to twenty percent of Israelis describe themselves as ultra-Orthodox or Orthodox. The rest of Israelis describe themselves as traditionally observant. It is important to remember, however, that even the more liberal of Israeli Jews tend to be more observant than their counterparts in America.

Other that that, most Jews are pretty much concerned with the same things when they're in temple: acknowledging the presence of God, honoring our past and our heritage, and working toward a brighter future for all people.

Today, ironically, there are some close ties between the Hasidism and the more liberal movements of Judaism, and one of those things is Kabbalah. The founder of Hasidism, the Ba'al Shem Tov, also wrote one of the major Kabbalah works, and more liberal Jews who have been seeking a way back into the religion of their heritage enjoy a common bond: the study of Kabbalah.

Despite the many denominations, I will make a generalization of Jews right now: They love to discuss their beliefs and try to figure out what certain Torah portions mean. They believe that if they figure out exactly what God means by a specific word or Torah portion, then they will be that much closer to God.

And speaking of how much Jews love to discuss things, here's what Kabbalah is:

Bearing in mind that Jews have spent more than two thousand years discussing and kibitzing, you won't be surprised to learn that before the 18th century, it was generally believed that the ideal way to get close to God was to become as scholarly as possible. The most observant and highly respected Jews would read and discuss Torah passages for hours at a time.

Kabbalah means "to receive," and it doesn't refer to a specific book. It means to receive a specific way of learning and understanding the books that are important to Jews. These books are called, to Jews, *TNK* or *Tanach*, which consists of the Torah (the first five books of the Bible—Genesis, Exodus, Leviticus, Numbers, and Deuteronomy); *Nevi'im*, or Prophets (the next series of books); and *Ktuvim*, the writings from Psalms to 2 Chronicles. Jews do not refer to these books as the Old Testament, because they do not recognize the New Testament. Tanach is simply an acronym for the abbreviation of these thirty-nine books.

Some other important Jewish texts include the *Mishnah* and *Gemara*, which constitute the Talmud. These texts discuss how Jews are supposed to live their lives—they are the laws of Judaism, as opposed to the beliefs and the stories of the Jews.

These traditions could not be written down, but they were learned by word of mouth—from teacher to student. Another important tool of study for Jews is the Midrash, rabbinic teachings that are attached to the text of the Bible, almost like annotations.

In the mid–18th century, a man named Israel ben Eliezer (now more often called the Ba'al Shem Tov) began to gain influence by teaching that a more mystical approach to learning was truly the best way to experience God. He founded the Hasidic school of Judaism. All of this talking and all of this reading, he felt, weren't enough to get close to God. There had to be something more.

Although many books of his teachings exist, the *Besht* (an acronym for Ba'al Shem Tov) himself wrote no books, perhaps because his teachings emphasized the fact that even a simple, uneducated peasant could approach God (a radical idea in its time). He emphasized prayer; the observance of commandments; and ecstatic, personal, mystical experiences.

The very first work of Kabbalah, *Sefer Yetzirah*, The Book of Formation, is attributed to Abraham. The *Sefer Yetzirah* is a small and concise book. The text was deliberately written in a fashion that would be meaningless to those without an extensive background in the Tanach and Midrash (the oral teaching of the Torah). The first commentaries on this book were written in the 10th century, and the text itself is quoted as early as the sixth century.

Seven generations after Abraham, we received the Torah on Mount Sinai, which includes:

1. The laws and will of God. These laws express the will of God for our ultimate and absolute good in this world and all worlds.

2. The Kabbalah, the inner dimension, the soul of the Torah, which is the comprehension of the secrets of Creation.

In approximately 100 C.E., Rabbi Shimon bar Yochai (Rashbi) was given the power and permission from Heaven to fully reveal and explicitly discuss and teach the intricacies of Kabbalah. He explained the functions of all the *sefirot*, which we will explain in Chapter One, and how they manifest in every verse of the Torah and in every phenomenon of nature. The great classic text of Kabbalah, written by Rashbi, is the *Sefer Hazohar*, the Book of Brilliance. It includes Rashbi's revelations of Kabbalah, as taught to his disciples.

The next book of Kabbalah is the *Zohar*, the Book of Radiance, which first became popular in 13th-century Spain. The Zohar is at least three large volumes, more than a dozen when a commentary is included. It is a kind of midrash, an imaginative commentary on the Torah, in which any verse or word can inspire pages of teachings and stories.

Since its first appearance in Spain, the Zohar has been associated with a rabbi named Moshe de Leon, although no one is sure if he was the author, or if his students simply wrote down his teachings.

The Zohar circulated in loose pages. Toward the late 1500s, it was arranged to fit weekly Torah portions and put into print. It eventually became the central text of the Kabbalistic tradition and future Kabbalists wrote their commentaries to the book.

Over the next couple of centuries, Jews and other Kabbalists accepted the Zohar as a holy book.

Kabbalah says that the Torah is a code, like a cryptogram. Students are supposed to read it carefully—noticing the numbers, the letters, and the names of the people who are mentioned—to uncover the secret of life. That's because in Hebrew, letters and numbers are the same (for example, an aleph is "a" and also "1"), so those same letters and numbers add up to or symbolize other words and ideas. A Kabbalah student is instructed to notice patterns and similarities that seem like the most complicated and yet highly significant puzzle that has ever been created.

In fact, some people think that untangling these secrets will bring students the secret of life.

Kabbalah and Pop Culture

Before we get into our discussion of what Kabbalah can do for us, I want to discuss Kabbalah's popularity today. As I was writing this, an article appeared in *People* magazine discussing Kabbalah's popularity in Hollywood. Winona Ryder, an actress of Jewish ancestry, wore a red ribbon around her wrist during her shoplifting trial, since it is an old Jewish superstition that a red ribbon will keep away the evil eye. Demi Moore and Madonna also wear red ribbons.

Superstitions are not about Kabbalah, and Kabbalah is not about superstitions or magic. In fact, Kabbalah isn't magic. To consider it magic is to buy into long-standing prejudices against Jews. Think about the Salem witch trials. The women accused of witchcraft were living in a repressive, highly religious community. Their heresy was not just against the community, but also against God, according to those who judged them.

For centuries, Jews have been accused of witchcraft. And, although this stereotype may no longer be prevalent, to imagine that Kabbalah writings or, worse, the Torah, will somehow allow you to cast a spell or find out the secret of living forever is a misuse of the power of Kabbalah.

Only God has the power to change the course of people's lives. To imagine that anyone, as a person, has a power he or she can draw from to help or hurt someone is incorrect. Kabbalah teaches us to connect with God through meditation, learning, and thoughtfulness. It does not offer anyone the ability to cast spells, live forever, or prevent death. Anyone can study Kabbalah and anyone can learn from Kabbalah study, but Kabbalah isn't the secret of life. It is the secret of getting closer to God.

Some people relate tarot cards to the Kabbalah. The link between Kabbalah and tarot was simply—and not divinely—created by A. E. Waite. A student of Kabbalah, Waite designed a well-known and popular tarot card deck (Rider-Waite) using the Ten Sefirot (see Chapter One).

It's important to know that God (at least according to Kabbalah) did not intend for us to relate tarot to the Tanach. Tarot, for one thing, uses a lot of symbolism that isn't related to God and that is strictly prohibited by the Ten Commandments.

Second, God doesn't ask us to predict the future. God asks us, instead, to do good deeds, remain connected to the Divine, and trust in our future with the Almighty.

That said, our language, the one you and I share as 21st-century readers, is familiar with tarot and astrology, much more so than it is with Torah. We understand what it means to say someone is a lot like an Aries or that the devil card in tarot came up during a reading. Because it is my goal to make Kabbalah accessible, I have used these references in my writing, as well as the language and sayings of the Torah.

Why I Wrote This Book

There is no doubt that to study Kabbalah, you must read the Tanach and study with a learned teacher. There is no doubt that Kabbalah cannot be taught outside of the context of Jewish history. As I mentioned earlier, I do not believe that Kabbalah is the secret to anything more than what it purports to be, which is a specific, connective level of Judaism.

However, I do believe in being realistic. The reality of life today is that few people know Hebrew. And yet, at the same time, numerous non-Jews have an interest in Judaism and Kabbalah. It's not easy to begin to study Torah, and it's not easy to make a direct connection from today's numerous spiritual offerings—such as yoga, meditation, and a belief in God rather than in organized religion—to a practical study of Torah.

At the same time, I had a journey from Reform Jew to Buddhist to Kabbalist that I honor and respect. I was thrilled to find the meditation-oriented language I "spoke" in my religious heritage. This book respectfully combines both of those languages; in fact, if I could have written this book in the Yiddish-accented tongue of my relatives, I would have, because I know the words sound mystical, and I would love it if they could also sound day-to-day, down-to-earth, and real.

Therefore, this book is, I hope, both a beginning and an end. It is a beginning for those of you who are new to Judaism and Kabbalah, and it is an end for those of you who have been searching for a way to blend, as I have, my religious upbringing with my adult spiritual practices. I hope it will lead you to other books and deeper study. At the same time, I hope it helps you feel, just momentarily, as you read each tip, at peace in the world and connected to God.

The Secret of Life

"Salt adds flavor to food, though it is not itself a food. The same is true of the Kabbalah. In itself it is hardly comprehensible, and it is tasteless, but it adds flavor to the Torah."

—Rabbi Schneur Zalman of Lyadi

It is easy, living in this day and age of exploration and open-mindedness, to imagine that all we are going to learn in this particular book will take us—symbolically—into the future and away from the past. But that is not my intention. It isn't that I want to bring anyone into a state of mind that keeps us bound to outmoded traditions. Nor am I saying that, if you are comfortable with your belief that the Tanach is more metaphor than reality, then you should change your mind.

All I'm saying is that while you read this information—this collection of information about names, letters, numbers, and the Jewish calendar—I hope you will not look at it as magic, but rather as a way to connect with the true meaning of Jewish spiritual teachings. You do not have to be Jewish, you do not have to be a specific type of Jew, but I would like you to keep these teachings in the context of Judaism—which is, as I wrote earlier—a belief that God exists, that God is all-powerful, and that God is one.

Some Kabbalah students will tell you that with Kabbalah knowledge you will learn how to create a golem (a man-made person, like Frankenstein), while others will say that if you come to understand Kabbalah fully you will never die. I think that is all ridiculous.

I will tell you right up front that the secret of life does not involve eternal life. Or never aging. Or finding true love. Or becoming rich. Or being famous. Or any of the things so many of us strive to accomplish in our lives today.

The secret of life is drawing closer to God.

And that is what Kabbalah offers us—the secret to drawing closer to God in every moment of our lives, whether we're fully mindful and conscious or whether we're feeling mystical and transcendent. Kabbalah study gives us the tools we need to reach God on every level—mind, body, and spirit.

CHAPTER ONE

Ein Sof
and the
Tree of Life

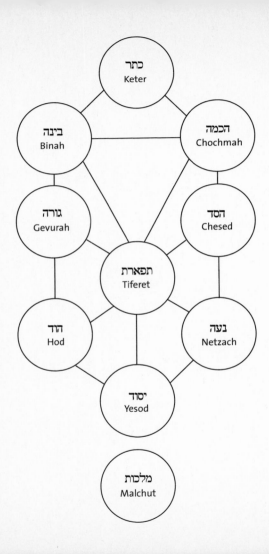

What You Know of God Is Only
That Which You Can Conceive

The first two basic ideas of Kabbalah are *Ein Sof* and the *sefirot*. *Ein Sof* is, basically, the energy of the universe. God is called *Ein Sof*, which means "without end" in Hebrew. This name symbolizes God's transcendence of boundaries in time and space. *Ein Sof* represents the true hidden essence of God, which is entirely unknown to humans.

I think back to the times, when I was little, when I tried to imagine how God could be "bigger" than the universe. It's unfathomable, isn't it? Kabbalah acknowledges this mystery and, at the same time, allows for the creation of the universe by God. Kabbalah interprets the creation of the universe as a contraction and expansion of God's energy—not unlike the big bang theory.

Kabbalah states that *Ein Sof* contracted His divine energy and created a vacuum. In this vacuum, He created worlds in which we exist and know, making God "visible" to us (on a spiritual level). *Ein Sof* interacts with the world through ten manifestations, or emanations, known as the Ten Sefirot. The *sefirot* are ten divine attributes of God, which help create and infuse *Ein Sof*. *Ein Sof* and the *sefirot* are each part of the other. "It is they and they are it," Kabbalists say.

In other words, this world, and its ten emanations, is a dwelling place for God's Infinite Light and His absolute essence. What we know of God we can use to create our best selves. As the Sages say, "Just as God is merciful, so must you be merciful." God has attributes that are manifest and revealed in reality. In fact, Kabbalists believe that God created this space and energy and the people within it to behold himself, "and it was good."

The Ten Sefirot are the ten archetypal attributes or characteristics of God that human beings can know. *Ein Sof* itself is something we cannot know because of our human limitations of imagination. When the Jewish soul becomes one with this wisdom and comprehension, his or her whole life pattern is changed, from the consciousness of the mind, to the emotions of the heart, to the person's behavior. From experiencing this enlightenment, we transcend the world and begin to know God on an entirely new dimension—that is the point of Kabbalah.

All Human Knowledge of God Is Really of the Ten *Sefirot*

The Kabbalist Tree of Life has ten qualities which relate to each of the *sefirot*, as well as twenty-two branches connecting them. The *sefirot* are not separate ideas. In fact, there is great significance to the position of these various attributes and their interconnectedness. They are intimately a part of God, and yet they are in contact with the universe in a way that *Ein Sof* is not.

The good and evil that we do resonates through the *sefirot* and affects the entire universe, up to and including God Himself. There is a flow of divine power and blessing from one *sefirah* to another, finally reaching *Malchut*, which is the presence of God in the world.

By acknowledging and being mindful of the Ten *Sefirot*, we can know God in our world. They are:

- *Keter* – Crown. *Keter* represents equilibrium as a force residing at the axis of a fulcrum. In *Keter*, the two opposing forces of the Tree of Life (expansion and contraction) exist in potential, not in reality.

- *Chochmah* – Wisdom. The father of the Tree of Life, *Chochmah* is the point where the emanation from the *Ein Sof* starts to move into our world.

- *Binah* – Understanding. The mother of the Tree of Life, *Binah* refers to God's analytical thought. With the seed of *Chochmah*, *Binah* conceived and gave birth to the seven lower *sefirot*.

- *Chesed* – Kindness. Created by the union of *Chochmah* and *Binah*, *Chesed* is the life-giving force that manifests itself in humans and in the universe. *Chesed* represents love and generosity.

- *Gevurah* – Strength. With the power to dispense judgment, mete out punishment, and exert control, *Gevurah* limits the abundance of mercy (*Chesed*).

- *Tiferet* – Beauty. The only *sefirah* connected to all the others on the Tree of Life, *Tiferet* balances *Chesed* and *Gevurah*. It is the inner core, a perfect balance.
- *Netzach* – Victory. *Netzach* represents the passion and energy of Creation.
- *Hod* – Awe. *Hod* represents truthful thought and limits *Gevurah* with honesty and introspection.
- *Yesod* – Foundation. *Yesod* represents the union of action, thought, passion, and truthfulness.
- *Malchut* – Kingdom (as in the physical existence of God's emanations). It is through *Malchut* that *Ein Sof*'s emanations reach the physical plane. *Malchut* is you as you are, right now. "*Malchut*, which is the presence of God in the world."

Sections of the Tree of Life

In addition to the Ten *Sefirot*, the Tree of Life is made up of several sections. Each has its own profound significance:

The First Triad

Ein Sof emanates, and *Keter* is His light. The emanation divides into the father and mother (*Chochmah* and *Binah*). *Chochmah* is the will to expand, the chaotic force, and the driving need to live, reproduce, and learn. *Binah* accepts this force and modifies it. Without *Binah*, *Chochmah* would expand out of control, and life would be impossible. Without *Chochmah*, *Binah* would maintain perfect stasis; there would be no life at all. These two *sefirot*, combined with *Keter* (the beginning point), form the supernal triad. Together they represent knowledge, wisdom, and understanding.

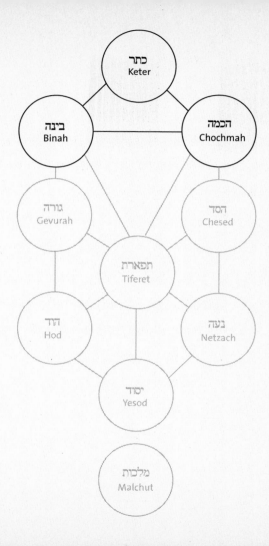

The Second Triad

Chesed, *Gevurah*, and *Tiferet* represent the second triad, that of God's moral power. It explains the idea that God judges us. In the meantime, these three qualities (*Chesed* is loving-kindness, *Gevurah* is judgment, and *Tiferet* is beauty) allow us to, in term, offer these qualities to others.

The Veil of Parochet

Below the second triad lies the Veil of Parochet. This is the separation of the second triad from the rest of the Tree of Life. The second triad, while a more human and approachable reflection of the supernal triad, is still too archetypical for humans to experience directly.

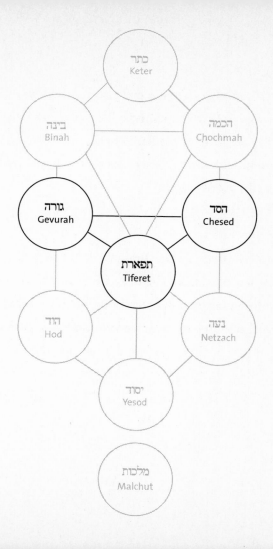

The Third Triad

Netzach, *Hod*, and *Yesod* represent the third triad, which is the material universe in its many forms. This triad is composed of the most turbulent and human of the *sefirot*. The third triad describes our everyday emotions and experiences. It is from this third triad that *Malchut*, the tenth *sefirah*, is created.

The Abyss

There is a gap between the supernal triad and the rest of the *sefirot* on the Tree of Life. This is the separation between the potential of the universe and our thoughts. The Abyss represents the gap between thought and action. Imagine if you acted out every single thought that appeared in your mind or if every possibility that exists in the world suddenly became reality. That is what life would be like without The Abyss. We need—and the universe requires—nothingness.

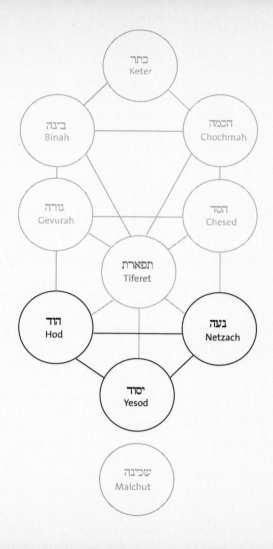

The Four Worlds

You can meditate on each of the *sefirot* on its own, but you have another option. Kabbalists have grouped them together into worlds, too, that correspond to levels of our own existence.

Atzilut:

The World of Proximity and Emanation. It is a world that exists on a gut level, but not in words or reality. It's the way you know things that you cannot express or fully understand.

Beriyah:

The World of Creation. Ideas and our creations from those ideas emanate from this level of existence.

Yetzirah:

The World of Our Mind. This can either bloom into creative thought, or be polluted by repeated obsessions and habits.

Assiyah:

The World of Action. We take our ideas and our creativity and put them into action in this plane.

The Paths of the *Sefirot*

Each path linking two *sefirah* has its own significance. Although the *sefirah* were not created with tarot cards in mind, the reverse is true: tarot cards have been created with these pathways. I have included the Rider-Waite variation in this section for your understanding, but I caution you against imagining that Kabbalists would relate these concepts to anything other than the Torah.

I've written a meditation for each pathway. To me, a student of Buddhism, Yoga, and Chakras, these meditations correspond to our energy levels and our spiritual focus.

Remember, the intention of each meditation is to become closer to God, the creator of the energy of the universe.

Joining Yesod *and* Malchut

"The Path of Administrative Intelligence"

Tarot Card: The World

Celestial Body: Saturn

Color: Black

The path that connects *Yesod* and *Malchut* is the one on which the emanations of the entire tree is transmitted toward the physical plane. All divine forces combine to make their mark in the sensory world on this path. The tarot card associated with this path depicts a virginal Goddess dancing with a serpent before the background of the heavenly wheel.

Meditation: I am at one with the energy of the world.

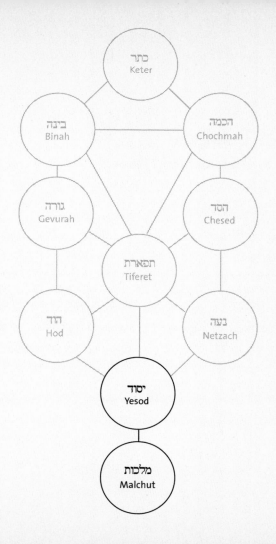

Joining Hod *and* Malchut
"The Path of Perpetual Intelligence"

Tarot Card: Judgment
Celestial Body: Pluto
Color: Vermilion

Combining ambition and reality, this path signifies perpetual change in oneself. The tarot card is "the symbol of unlimited possibilities."

Meditation: My intention and my focus create positive energy.

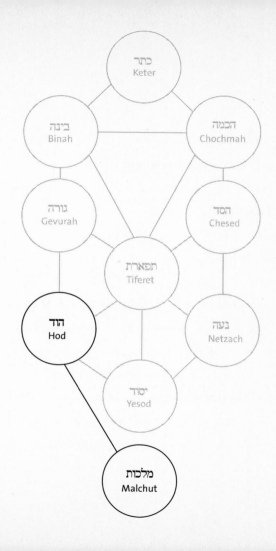

Joining Hod *and* Yesod
"The Path of Collecting Intelligence"

Tarot Card: The Sun
Celestial Body: Sun
Color: Golden yellow

This path connects *Hod*'s concentrated mind-forms with the amplifying magnetic images of *Yesod*. It indicates how to achieve enlightenment and consciously create our existence on Earth. The tarot card features the sun shining upon all Creation as a symbol of the power of life.

Meditation: I open my spirit to all possibilities.

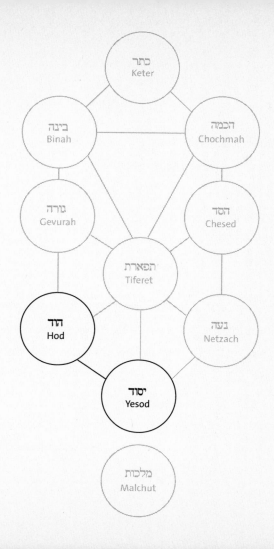

Joining Netzach *and* Malchut
"The Path of Corporeal Intelligence"

Tarot Card: The Moon
Celestial Body: Moon
Color: Buff

This is the path of our physical heritage, stemming from biological evolution and from the soul's specific organization of the body during incarnation. The Moon symbolizes physical birth and death and the cycles of the moon.

Meditation: My body is in synch with the energy of *Ein Sof*.

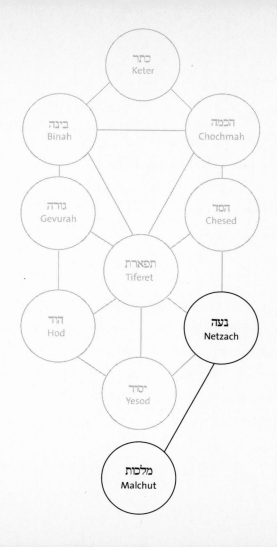

Joining Netzach *and* Yesod
"The Path of Constituting Intelligence"

Tarot Card: The Emperor
Celestial Body: Uranus/Saturn
Color: Red

This is the divine link between mind and matter, with an inflow of *Netzach*'s collective channels and archetypes. This path breaks up the mechanisms of *Yesod* to enable a greater freedom based on higher principles. The Emperor symbolizes rulership of the mind over nature, creativity, and stability, as well as a sense of responsibility.

Meditation: I control my creative energy with thoughtfulness.

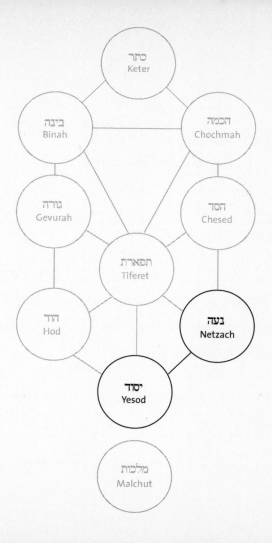

Joining Netzach *and* Hod
"The Path of Exciting Intelligence"

Tarot Card: The Tower
Celestial Body: Mars
Color: Bright red

Between the imbalances of *Hod* (form) and *Netzach* (function) you can achieve equilibrium through proper creative energy. The Tower illustrates great creation.

Meditation: I create with an understanding of form and function, need and desire.

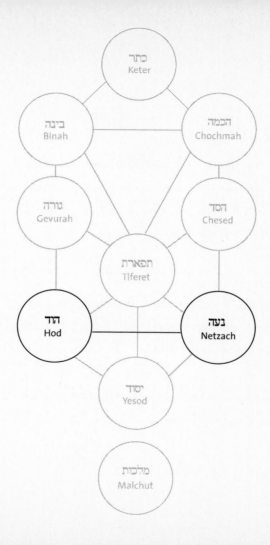

Joining Tiferet *and* Hod
"The Path of Renovating Intelligence"

Tarot Card: The Devil
Celestial Body: Saturn
Color: Black

This path takes our perceptions and communicates them to us in a way that we can easily understand. In tarot, the Devil can be good or bad, depending on what it lies next to, i.e., its intention.

Meditation: There is no inherent negative. I take all that comes to me and turn all events and choices into opportunity.

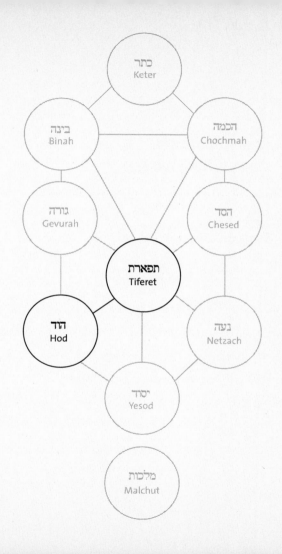

Joining Tiferet *and* Yesod
"The Path of Tentative Intelligence"

Tarot Card: Art
Celestial Body: Jupiter
Color: Yellow

The path between *Tiferet* and *Yesod* forms the trunk of the Tree of Life. This journey encompasses a spiritual undertaking and maps out a route from the mundane to the celestial. In the process, we internalize the exterior, cruder forces that exist to refine impure elements.

Meditation: My life energies direct me to the divine.

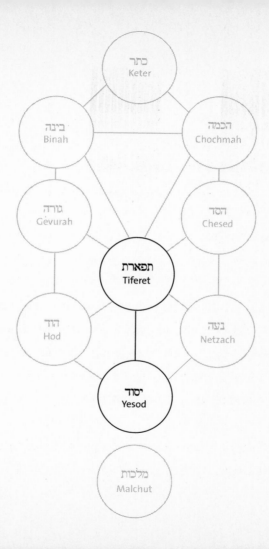

Joining Tiferet *and* Netzach

"The Path of Imaginative Intelligence"

Tarot Card: Death
Celestial Body: Mars
Color: Brown

Tiferet is a place where opposites meld and where integrations and manifestations occur. On this path it blends with *Netzach*, a place where perfect forms are transformed, re-polarized, and made accessible to the human mind. The tarot card related to this pathway is Death, a rebirth for the soul without the constraint of a physical death.

Meditation: I embrace change as the energy of life.

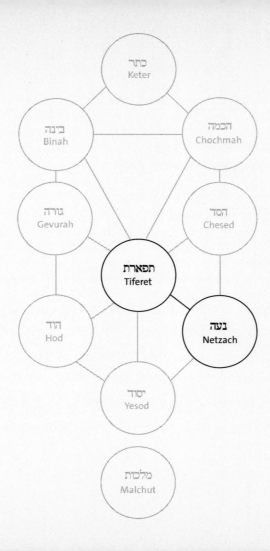

Joining Gevurah *and* Hod
"The Path of Stable Intelligence"

Tarot Card: The Hanged Man
Celestial Body: Neptune
Color: Sea green

This is a link from *Gevurah*'s celestial law to *Hod*'s encapsulation of energy into forms. The tarot trump the Hanged Man suggests a sacrifice, devotion, and an acceptance of destiny.

Meditation: I accept the day-to-day reality of life as a pathway to the Divine.

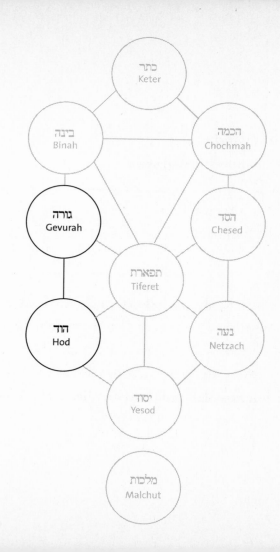

Joining Gevurah *and* Tiferet
"The Path of Faithful Intelligence"

Tarot Card: Adjustment
Celestial Body: Venus
Color: Blue

This path relates to the knowledge we gain from reinventing ourselves.

Meditation: When my spiritual growth asks that I let go of past beliefs and associations, I honor them, but I move ahead with faith.

Joining Chesed *and* Netzach
"The Path of Conciliating Intelligence"

Tarot Card: Fortune
Celestial Body: Jupiter
Color: Dark blue

This pathway takes the justice of *Chesed* with *Netzach*, the *sefirah* of acquisitiveness. Often that which we aspire to is unattainable, even undesirable, when viewed from a cosmic perspective. Fortune, its related tarot card, demonstrates that there are no universal ambiguities.

Meditation: What I want is not as important as appreciating what I have.

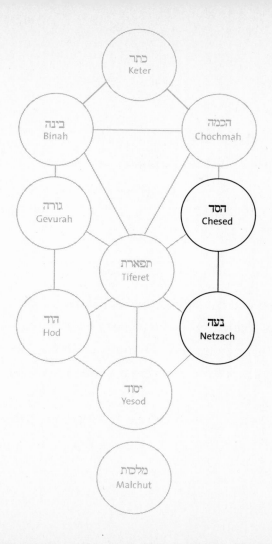

Joining Chesed *and* Tiferet
"The Path of Willful Intelligence"

Tarot Card: The Hermit
Celestial Body: Mercury
Color: Slate gray

This path connects *Chesed*, the archetype of mercy, love, and justice, with *Tiferet*, the melting pot of the Tree of Life. The companion tarot trump, the Hermit, facilitates our comprehension of *Hod* as a path to emotional maturity and inner depth.

Meditation: I strive to love others as part of my spiritual growth.

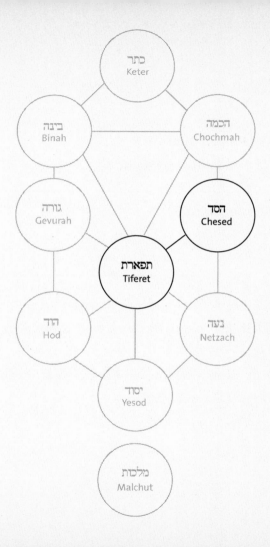

Joining Chesed *and* Gevurah
"The Path of Spiritual Intelligence"

Tarot Card: Strength/Lust
Celestial Body: Sun
Color: Deep purple

This path symbolizes the seduction that happened within the Garden of Eden. It is related to the tarot trump, Lust.

Meditation: It is my responsibility to balance my physical desires with the Divine energy.

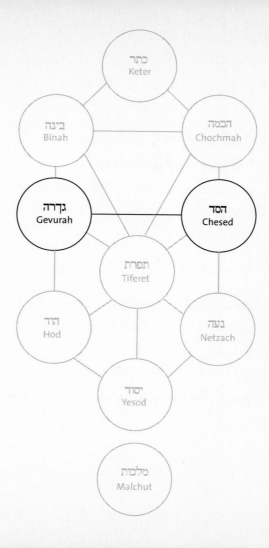

Joining Binah *and* Gevurah

"The Path of Influencing Intelligence"

Tarot Card: The Chariot
Celestial Body: Moon
Color: Maroon

This is the path of destiny between *Binah*, the Mother of the universe, and *Gevurah*, the arbiter of Divine Law. The Chariot symbolizes divine journeys.

Meditation: Male and female energy are in concert within me.

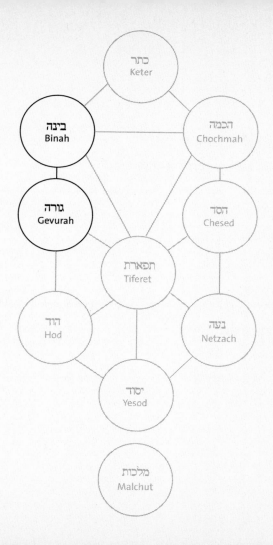

Joining Binah *and* Tiferet
"The Path of Disposing Intelligence"

Tarot Card: The Lovers
Celestial Body: Mercury
Color: Mauve

This path brings us together with our beloved, symbolized with the tarot trump, the Lovers.

Meditation: My soulmate exists and God will bring us together.

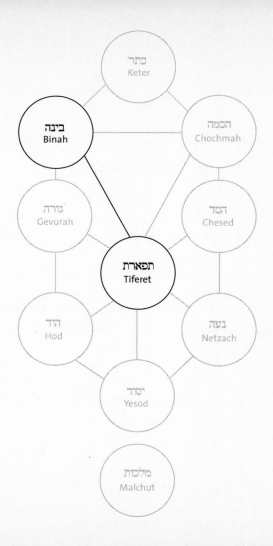

Joining Chochmah *and* Chesed
"The Path of Triumphal Intelligence"

Tarot Card: The Hierophant
Celestial Body: Venus
Color: Indigo

This path unites the process of learning and teaching Divine Law. In tarot, this path is related to the Hierophant. He passes on the divine knowledge of the Priestess.

Meditation: It is my duty to learn, and then to teach others what I know.

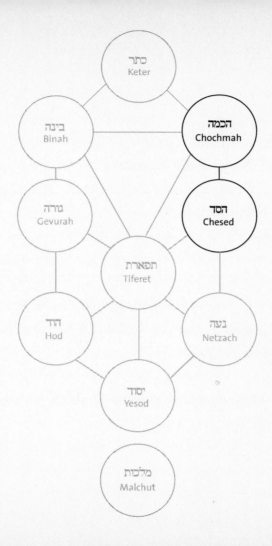

Joining Chochmah *and* Tiferet
"The Path of Natural Intelligence"

Tarot Card: The Star
Celestial Body: Mars
Color: Light blue

This is the masculine path, characterized by the Star tarot card. It enables the seeker to understand hidden truths found outside his or her sphere of reality.

Meditation: I know more than what I can see with my eyes and hear with my ears.

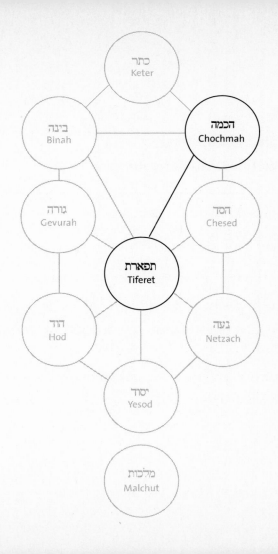

Joining Binah *and* Chochmah
"The Path of Illuminating Intelligence"

Tarot Card: The Empress
Celestial Body: Venus
Color: Blue

This is the path of love and fertility. The Goddess of Love is seen in the tarot card illustrating the potential of our romantic energy.

Meditation: My creations are expressions of Divine love.

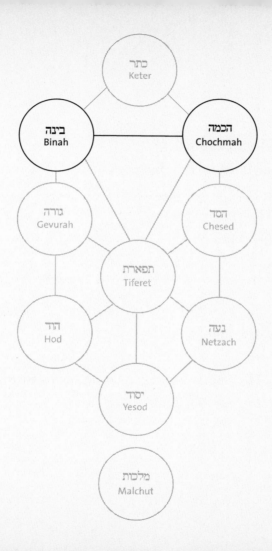

Joining Keter *and* Tiferet
"The Path of Uniting Intelligence"

Tarot Card: The High Priestess
Celestial Body: Moon
Color: Silver

This path symbolizes the camel, an animal that can care for itself when it is isolated and alone.

Meditation: My ability to self-care and self-nurture is God's way of showing me that I am never alone.

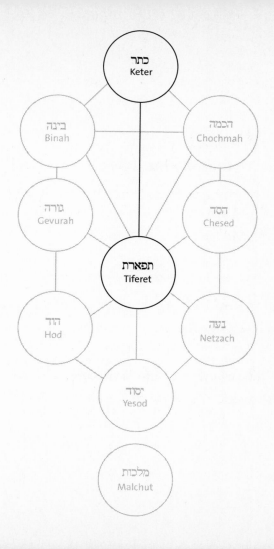

Joining Keter *and* Binah

"The Path of Transparent Intelligence"

Tarot Card: The Magus
Celestial Body: Mercury
Color: Purple

This path directs the spirit flowing out of *Keter* and molds it into the great womb of *Binah*.

Meditation: The rhythm of life is proof of Divine energy.

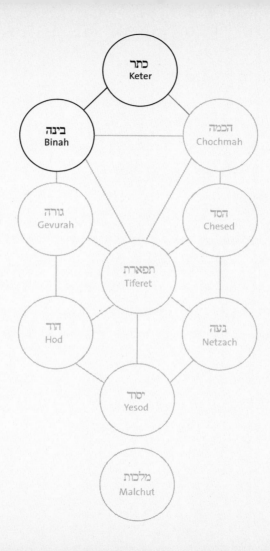

Tree of Life Affirmations

To bring us closer to the idea of *Ein Sof*, we will meditate on the *sefirot* in two ways. One is an "I am" statement. This type of affirmation moves you from an "I wish" or "I want to be" state of mind to a more positive paradigm. It moves you from a state of desire to a state of being.

The second type of affirmation puts you in a secure place within the world around you. Very often, when we are at our most spiritual, we feel isolated from people even while we feel deeply connected to God. Let's face it: Most of us don't talk about our beliefs with our family and friends. So, these affirmations support the idea that you, like those around you, are on a spiritual quest.

KETER AFFIRMATION
"I am divine."

The point of studying the *sefirot* is to understand the levels at which we can strive to connect with God. What we perceive is not all that God is, but because our perception of God is literally all we can know of Him at this moment, it is enough.

Of all the qualities of the *sefirot*, the most important one is knowing that, as God is divine, so are we. If we can conceive of the Divine, then we can conceive of being divine.

Now, in my eyes, this doesn't mean that we strive to be perfect. We aren't perfect, and we aren't meant to be perfect. Personally, I think that striving to be perfect is a good way to simply drive yourself nuts. Instead, I think we should strive, at every moment, to connect with God.

That connection is our method of being divine. Although we can't reach perfection—or even fully understand what perfection and God are—we can always have the intention of being closer to God. And that intention will remind us that there is a part of us that is divine.

CHOCHMAH AFFIRMATION
"I am one path of the world's entire existence."

"This isn't right," we say to ourselves when things don't go our way. We want what others have or we want our lives to be different. But, the *Chochmah sefirah* reminds us that the world is the way it is and we are meant to be at peace with that.

This is not to say that you should sit complacently by when injustice is brought to your attention. Nor should you let people walk all over you or not strive to accomplish all the things you want to accomplish. On the contrary, God wants you to have the intention, as we discussed above, to connect with His divine light.

Therefore, if things appear not to be going your way, then perhaps the problem is that God's intention is for you to follow a different path, and perhaps that path is going to bring you more happiness, i.e., in closer contact with God, than the plan you have for yourself.

BINAH AFFIRMATION
"My being is aligned with the universe."

I live far from my family and friends and, because of that, I often feel not only physically isolated, but also spiritually isolated. Because I've traveled so far from home—alone—so often, I consider myself an expert on loneliness.

At the same time, I also consider myself an expert on connection. Because I am far from home and because I often feel lonely, I have to find ways to connect and feel connected, even if there aren't people around for me to connect with easily. Therefore, I have found quick and easy ways to connect to God by connecting to the universe. First, shut off the TV. While the characters on TV can seem to counteract loneliness, they don't. They make you lonelier. Shut off the stereo and the radio.

Now, go outside. Find a park or a beach or a mountain or anything natural. Look around. Take some deep breaths. Look at the sky. Look at the earth. Don't think. Just absorb.

You are part of this. Right here. Right now. You exist. And it's all good.

CHESED AFFIRMATION
"God offers us all peace of mind."

It is always a choice to live in a healthy frame of mind. Sometimes disturbing things happen and sometimes we have trouble disconnecting from unpleasant thoughts or memories.

But, God always offers us a way out—and that is through our connection with Him.

When you're having trouble controlling your negative thoughts or your negative behavior patterns, you can try simply focusing your attention on your connection with God. Just like any ability to change a habit, this can take a while, but it really does work.

Once you're focused on this intention and this relationship, then other issues and problems take a backseat to the goodness. Problems don't disappear, but they do get put into their proper perspective.

GEVURAH AFFIRMATION
"My struggles are gifts from God."

Sometimes life is rough: We are alone, we feel rejected, we fail. And this is often when we curse God. We get angry at Him for making us conscious of our own shortcomings. The important thing, in these moments, is to remember that struggles are gifts from God, just as all easy-to-recognize gifts are. God is offering us the opportunity to grow, to be better, and to connect with Him through humility, rather than through pride.

This isn't to say that God loves us when we fail more than He loves us when we succeed. It's simply to say that God is there for us, to support us when we fail, and He hopes we'll both appreciate Him and remember Him when we manage to do well, too.

TIFERET AFFIRMATION
"I am part of other people's divine plans."

I have a friend who never hesitates to tell me how much she loves me. She always lets me know that I matter in her life.

Hardly anyone else does that. I know I matter to other people—I am someone's child, someone's sibling, someone's parent, and other people's friend. When I have the open heart to love myself, I am able to remember that I exist in other people's lives and that, sometimes, I'm actually a good part of their lives. What a gift that is.

If you have trouble remembering that you matter, connect to God. I believe that when you walk around feeling yourself connected to His spirit, you will more easily remember that others are part of His light, too, and that when you connect to Him, you are connecting to others. And vice versa. When you connect with others, you are connecting with Him.

NETZACH AFFIRMATION
"What I give is my gift to the universe."

As I was writing this particular section of the book, my little boy got a cold and, instead of being able to work one afternoon, I had to stay on my couch and take care of my young son.

As I sat inside on a gorgeous sunny day, unable to do my work and also unable to go outside and enjoy the day, I looked down at my son and thought about all the days that my own mother took care of me when I was sick. These are some of my fondest memories: the ginger ale, lying on the couch, having toast. Of course, it wasn't the particulars that really mattered, it was the idea that someone was taking care of me.

And now, I take care of my son.

We think of these moments and choices as gifts to the individuals— and maybe, when we are feeling generous and aware—as gifts to ourselves. God would have us believe, too, that they are gifts to Him and His universe. When I am kind, whether it's to my son or to a stranger, I am offering my love to the world God has given us all.

I want to point out, too, that I'm not talking about giving physical gifts. While it is certainly true that giving sometimes involves money or things, more often than not, giving involves the gift of time, attention, and, in one form or another, love.

HOD AFFIRMATION
"I appreciate what others give me."

One of the best decisions I ever made was choosing to see everything that happens—even things that make me sad or angry—as gifts and opportunities. Now, I'm not saying I'm Pollyanna. I have a pretty volatile personality, if truth be told. And my first instinct—always—is to look at the negative. In fact, I'm pretty paranoid. I suspect everyone of plotting against me.

But, after my initial reaction, I make the conscious decision to think instead that God has chosen to give me this oppotrunity—via another person—for a reason. If I believe that God works through me, then I also must believe that God works through others.

Now, if you're following me here, this way of thinking may sound a little self-centered. As if God is directing the entire universe, people and all, to either reward me or challenge me. So, we need to take this one step further.

Kabbalah states that everything that happens and everything that is written either brings us closer to or further away from God. God puts challenges in front of us to allow us to prove ourselves, not as a test to receive His love, but as spiritual beings that strive to be closer to Him. Even if something challenging happens, you can be sure that God is at work and we are meant to be appreciative.

Oh, and here's a little more explanation: It isn't that God thinks people should suffer. In his wonderful book, *When Bad Things Happen to Good People*, Rabbi Harold Kushner explains that bad things happen so people can reach out to each other and realize the love—the ideal love—that is given to us by Him. Kushner also states that God isn't doing the bad stuff. He's allowing it, yes, but He's also, very often, giving people the option not to behave in ways that will bring pain to others.

When people don't have the goodness available within them to do the right thing, then I choose to believe that they are further from God (the goodness within their hearts and souls) than would make anyone happy. And I pray for them.

In that respect, I appreciate both the good and the challenges that I receive from others.

YESOD AFFIRMATION
"I am a part of a long chain of goodness."

As I mentioned earlier, I have fond memories of my mom taking care of me, and it warms my heart that one day my son will have fond memories of my caretaking, but we can extrapolate that feeling into an even longer ancestry.

God has offered His goodness to us since the beginning of time. In fact, God created this universe to offer us Himself.

Sometimes, as we look back over history, especially Jewish history, we can easily remember the more horrifying events, but overlook the triumphs, both large and small. And yet, at the same time, history (once again, especially Jewish history) offers us stories of heroes and heroines that can inspire us to greatness—whether it's having the courage to face anti-Semitism or simply making the decision to live a spiritual life in the face of people who don't encourage those choices. Whatever your particular challenge, history offers you someone to look up to and connect with.

Jews read the entire Tanach each year, the same portion each week of the year, to remind ourselves about our history and those who came before us. These stories teach us what it means to live in connection with God, but they also give us guideposts to help us feel that connection ourselves.

Sometimes the guideposts are lessons (or numbers or letters), but sometimes they are people, and it is often in the stories of these men and women that we can find our deepest familial connection.

MALCHUT AFFIRMATION
"I am part of a community that connects with God."

I have lived on both coasts of the United States and in the deep South. Very often, after each of my moves, someone in my family will ask, "Are there any Jews?" And the answer is always "yes."

But, I think, more importantly than there being Jews, there are always people who are also working on their connection to God. Some Jews, just like some Christians and some Muslims, certainly believe that there is only one route to this level of spirituality, but I am not one of those people. And, although Kabbalah professes to have the secret to all we are searching for, I will venture to say that it isn't one thing—one teaching or one belief— that will bring each of us to the secret of life. It is, instead, our desire, our intention, to do the right thing, and to embody loving-kindness.

When you look at the world with that frame of mind, when you meet people with that frame of reference, then you are able to connect with the basic goodness of all people and you don't worry about the categories in which we all find ourselves.

CHAPTER TWO

Language
and
Names

In Kabbalah, names are not just conventional means of communication. They are far more. Each one of them represents a concentration of energy and expresses a wealth of meaning that cannot be translated, or not fully at least, into speech or words. When the Kabbalists speak of Divine Names and letters, they are forced to use the twenty-two consonants of the Hebrew alphabet, in which the Torah is written, but they use meditation to reach the deeper, mystical meaning of the words.

Kabbalists believe that various combinations of the letters in God's name hold power. They also believe that God gave us the chapters of the Torah out of order, because, if we were to read the text in the correct order, we could raise the dead, among other miracles. Of course, not all of us have these same beliefs.

Out of all the names of God, the most holy one is the four-letter name known as the tetragrammaton. Even in prayer or study, this name is not pronounced the way it is written, out of awe and respect. It means "The Infiniteness." "He is and always was and always will be." When you connect yourself to infinity, you too can become infinite.

The letters are YHWH and they are unpronounceable. Many Kabbalists believe that by arranging and rearranging these letters they can decipher many secrets. The study of the power of these letters is quite torturous and difficult to make comprehensible on an everyday level. Nevertheless, the importance of names, and ultimately, letters, which we will get into in the next chapters, gives us some idea of how we should behave when using words and, especially, names.

Your Child's Name

When you name a child, you are being somewhat prophetic in defining the child's essence. Jewish tradition holds that there is divine assistance at the time of naming a baby. Choose the name carefully, and pray that the name is a benefit to the child. This is also true of a convert who chooses a Hebrew name.

In any language, the meaning of a name has some spiritual significance and may affect a personality. In naming children, it has always been the secular Jewish custom to give a Hebrew or Yiddish name, even if the child will eventually use a different name. This has legal ramifications in Jewish law regarding marriage documents, being called on in the synagogue for a special honor, and when being prayed for by others. Because a name is so important, it's possible that a name change will have an effect on the nature of the person and thereby alter the scales of justice in the spiritual realm.

Understand a Name's Significance

Names have many layers of meaning in Kabbalah. It's always a little difficult to understand that in English, because we don't automatically associate a name with its biblical meaning. For example, while we might associate the name Adam with the first man, most of us don't know that in Hebrew *adam* means "from the ground," which, to a Kabbalist, symbolizes much about our relationship with God's earth.

Likewise, the Hebrew word for Eve, *chava*, means "gives life." *Cain* means "to acquire," making it not surprising that he would feel so competitive with his brother and believe that much of what was around him belonged to him.

When the Tanach mentions a person, his or her name often symbolizes something about the passage in which the person exists. *Noah* means pacification, and that was his role—he pacified a God who was angry at the world for its sins.

Therefore, when choosing a name, especially a Torah-based name, think not only of its association with certain people, but also of its meaning as a word.

CHAPTER THREE

Letters and Numbers

Each letter in the Hebrew alphabet has a numerical value, just like Roman numerals, so Kabbalists not only consider a word's meaning, but also its actual value. When deciphering the Torah text, Kabbalists look for the relationships—I would almost call it a cross-pollination—among words, letters, and numbers.

In Hebrew, aleph through yod have the values 1 through 10. Yod through qoph have the values 10 through 100, counting by 10s. Qoph through taw have the values 100 through 400, counting by 100s. Final letters have the same value as their nonfinal counterparts.

Hebrew numerical values are not like numerology, and they aren't based on superstitions. The order of the letters is irrelevant to their value; letters are simply added to determine the total numerical value. The number 11 could be written as yod-aleph (10+1), aleph-yod (1+10), he-waw (5+6), daleth-daleth-gimel (4+4+3), or many other combinations of letters. The only significant oddity in this pattern is the numbers 15 and 16, which if rendered as 10+5 or 10+6 would be a name of God, so they are normally written as teth-waw (9+6) and teth-zayin (9+7).

Because of this system of assigning numerical values to letters, every word has a numerical value. There is an entire discipline of Jewish mysticism known as Gematria, which is devoted to finding hidden meanings in the numerical values of words. For example, the number 18 is very significant, because it is the numerical value of the word *chai*, meaning life. Jews often donate money or give gifts in values of 18 not only to be generous, but also to wish the recipient a long life.

As I mentioned, Kabbalists look for repeated numbers and their meanings when studying their spiritual texts. For example, the number 10 is a biggie: There were ten plagues in Egypt, Ten Commandments on Mount Sinai, ten statements of Creation, ten generations from Adam to Noah, and again from Noah to Abraham, and ten tests of Abraham.

Likewise, the letters themselves have symbolic deeper meanings, as well as numerical values. Jews, and Kabbalists especially, love letters and numbers because they help us better understand our relationship with our Creator.

Aleph

The Ten Commandments begin with the letter aleph: "I (Anochi) am your God who has taken you out of the land of Egypt, out of the house of bondage." This is symbolic because when God gives Moses the Torah, He is descending to the lower realm of humans. Then, in turn, Moses and his followers ascend. This is why aleph is formed by writing a yod above and a yod below with a waw bringing them together. Aleph reminds us that we have the means to bring ourselves closer to God just as God brings Himself to us.

Number: One
Biblical Reference: "God is One."
Torah Quote: *"Shema Yisrael, Adonai Elohainu, Adonai Echud."* Hear O Israel, The Lord is God, The Lord is One.

ALEPH MEDITATION
"Although I exist as myself, I am at one with God."

It's an odd balance—our desire to connect to the spiritual and our aware-ness of our human needs and qualities. But, when we are feeling at our most human, thinking about money, for example, or dreaming about fame, or wishing to be more attractive or whatever, it is at these precise moments that we should stop, sit, breathe, and consider our deepest self—the self that is connected to God.

It is only with this connection and sense of self that we can offer our-selves love. And then, in that Godlike spirit of love, we are able to see that not only do we not need many of these temporal desires, but also that we already have much of what we've been looking for.

Beth

This letter symbolizes God's house. Jews believe that God created a home for Himself when He created our universe, as well as human beings. We are divine souls that exist in human form. Here, the deepest passion of the Creator reaches fulfillment. The large beth is the first letter of the Torah and the beginning of Creation, *bereishit* (beginning), a word that also means "head of the house." Beth is written with three lines connected on the right side.

Number: Two

Biblical Reference: The animals boarded the Ark in twos.

Torah Quote: "They shall build me a Temple and I will dwell in them." In other words, God dwells in each of us (not in the Temple, but in those who recognize God).

BETH MEDITATION
"Life is a bracha (blessing)."

Most of us can complain for hours about the most mundane things—traffic, how hard we work, our weight—and yet few of us spend even a quarter of that time thanking God for what we have, which would include, when you come right down to it: traffic, how hard we work, and our weight—our very existence.

We cannot reach God when we are angry about our lot, whether it's God-given or humanly created. But, when we take the time to be grateful for what we have, we dwell in peace—and possibility. Working from a place of love and appreciation gives us the proper energy to make changes in our lives—if we so desire. If you don't like the traffic, your work, or your weight, you can do something about it, but only if you feel the serenity of happiness and thankfulness that will allow you to feed your God-connected spirit.

ג

Gimel

The word *gimel* comes from the word *gemul*, which means "give."
When we offer loving-kindness to others, we are bound to receive
God's love and God's gifts. The visual significance of gimel is a
waw with a yod as a foot, signifying a rich man running to bestow
good upon a poor man. In the end, God will give to us. We do not
give in order to be blessed by God; we give to emulate God.

Number: Three

Biblical References: Three primary elements of Creation: air,
water, and fire. Three Fathers: Abraham, Isaac, and Jacob. Three
divisions of Jewish souls: *Kohanim* (priests), *Leviim* (Levites), and
Israelites. Three parts of the Torah: The Five Books of Moses, the
Prophets, and the Writings.

Torah Quote: "Today in this world, do for them; tomorrow in the
Kingdom, receive the reward."

GIMEL MEDITATION
"I give to others as God gives to me."

When we feel our deepest connection to God, and when we feel all we have inside ourselves, then we are able to give to others. I don't mean the giving that involves money or advice, or the giving that is really about control. In other words, true giving is not about hoping to get something back, such as having someone change or like you or give to you in return.

No, I'm referring to the type of giving that is truly selfless. A smile, an appreciation for another person's true self, or helping someone else reach a goal that is important to him or her, but maybe not to you. This kind of giving is what God gives us: a chance and support. It is truly love and a divine light.

ד

Daleth

The word *daleth* means "door," and the door to God's house allows for the humble of spirit to enter. The door itself, the daleth, is the property of humility. Daleth is also the initial letter of the word *dirah*, "dwelling place," as in the phrase "[God's] dwelling place below." Thus, the full meaning of daleth is the door through which the humble enter into the realization of God's dwelling place below.

Number: Four

Biblical References: Four elements of the physical world: fire, air, water, and earth. Four worlds: *Atzilut*, *Beriyah*, *Yetzirah*, and *Assiyah*. Four matriarchs: Sarah, Rebecca, Rachel, and Leah. Jacob's four wives: Rachel, Leah, Bilhah, and Zilpah. The four sons and the four cups of wine at the Seder. Four feet of the divine throne: Abraham, Isaac, Jacob, and David. Four letters of God's name.

Torah Quote: "I will exalt you, God, for you have lifted me up."

DALETH MEDITATION
"You are not in control."

I am a big fan of the twelve-step program, Alcoholics Anonymous. I'm not an alcoholic, but once, at a low point in my life, I was able to read the twelve steps in a way that related to me. I struggled with the first step: "Recognize that we are powerless over our drinking." In my case, I wasn't powerless over drinking, but I was powerless over my situation, and yet I hated this idea—powerlessness just seemed, well, it literally seemed impossible to me. I am so powerful, so capable, so able to take care of everything in life.

But, you know what? Powerlessness, like humility, doesn't mean we are weak or incapable. It means that we must accept the reality that God has given us in our lives. It means we shouldn't dwell in delusion, but we should, instead, open the door to our need to connect to God in order to change and be divine.

ה

Heh

Heh means "take," but it closely relates to the word "gave," as it is used in the story of Jacob, who gave grain to his brothers without them knowing who he was. Upon his revelation to his brothers (and thereby to all of Egypt), his giving became that of the *heh*. Instead of grain he now gave seed. In other words, he now truly gave as God gives: generously and with the desire to let people grow and do for themselves.

Number: Five

Biblical References: Five origins of speech in the mouth. Five fingers of the hand. Five visible planets in the solar system. The five vanities in the opening verse of Ecclesiastes. Five levels of the soul. Five times "Bless God, my soul" in Psalms 103 and 104. Five books of Moses. Five voices at the giving of the Torah. Five times light in the first day of Creation. Five final letters.

Torah Quote: "We will do and understand

HEH MEDITATION
"What matters most is my connection to God."

More than anything, respect for the Kabbalah is a commitment to live a life of connection with God. It would be easier to live without concerning ourselves with doing the right thing or with the bigger picture. So many people are simply concerned with nonspiritual matters, such as making more money or looking as good as possible. Others believe their lives matter beyond the realm of the cultural and the here and now. Such people often see little outward reward for their beliefs and efforts. However, they have deep inward reward. They feel at peace and find meaning in little things, rather than looking for validation in external qualities.

ו

Waw

In the beginning, Infinite Light filled reality, and God contracted His light to create hollow empty space, allowing a place necessary for our existence. Into this vacuum God drew down a single line of light from the Infinite Source. This ray of light is the secret of the letter waw.

Number: Six

Biblical References: Six days of Creation and the six corresponding divine forces.

Torah Quote: "Let there be light and there was light."

WAW MEDITATION
"The spirit of God is within you."

While it is certainly not traditional Kabbalistic thinking, I can't help but ruminate on my favorite spiritual, "This little light of mine/I'm going to let it shine." I sing this song to my son, because I believe that one of the most important gifts I can bestow on him is the knowledge that he has a light inside him and that it is his job to let it shine, not just in this world, but also in God's glory. When we consider ourselves to be truly connected—not just metaphorically, but biologically—with God's light, then we can see how important it is that we be ourselves and love ourselves, just because we exist as part of God's Infinite Light.

ז

Zayin

Zayin is meaningful not because of its definition, but because it symbolizes the Sabbath, the seventh day of Creation (it is the seventh letter), as well as the number of seas and heavens.

Number: Seven

Biblical References: Seven days of Creation. Seven seas and seven heavens. Seven chambers of Paradise. Seven lamps of the menorah; seven categories of Jewish souls. Seven shepherds of Israel: Abraham, Isaac, Jacob, Moses, Aaron, Joseph, and David. Seven "eyes" of God watch over all Creation.

Torah Quote: "And on the seventh day He rested and saw that it was good."

ZAYIN MEDITATION

"I will nurture myself as God nurtures Himself."

Rest. It's extraordinary that in this day and age, rest is actually considered a luxury and an indulgence. People brag about how little sleep they get or about how tired they are. It's unfortunate, because good rest is so important that God talks about it! More than that, He actually does it. The Torah doesn't say, God worked for six days and then he ate doughnuts and drank coffee (like the rest of us do when we're tired). No, God rested.

I think the world would change for the better if we mimicked God not only in our desire to do good deeds and be divine, but if we also acknowledged our need to rest. Rest—and I don't even mean sleep, but rest, as in relaxation—makes us more creative, keeps us healthy, keeps our tempers in check, and keeps us young. And perhaps, speaking of God, perhaps when we dream we are closer to a consciousness that God wants us to reach.

In fact, dreams are mentioned very often in the Torah and, if you look at it that way, it's quite possible that our dream world is as real and as necessary as our waking life.

So don't be afraid to rest. God does it, too.

ח
Cheth

Cheth is the first letter of the Hebrew word for life, *chaim*. There are two levels of life: "essential life" and "life to enliven." In this interpretation, God is essential life—he is the beginning of our spirit and our physical beings. His energy is transmuted through us as "life," as in the state of being "enlivened."

Each of us has, within us, both essences: the essential life of God (or the light) as well as the ability to enliven life—the life that God has created all around us. To me, this is a revolutionary way to see ourselves: We hold within us the essence of God as well as the ability to illuminate His life.

Once you sit with this feeling and this belief, it can change the way you value yourself. You are of utmost importance to this life, because of what is within you and what you are capable of contributing to this world.

Number: Eight

Biblical References: "God is one in the seven heavens and the earth." The eighth day is the day of circumcision. The eight days of Chanukah.

Torah Quote: "The candle of God is the soul of man."

CHETH MEDITATION
"God's light is within others."

Previously, we talked about our light, but we need to remember that this light is God's light. He has given us a part of Himself to exist, and this gift is divine. We often forget, however, that God's light is in everyone. There is no part of God's world that is not a part of Him. Now, it is often difficult to see this light in people who are cruel, but it is our gift to God to treat those people respectfully, because we see their light and we honor it, as we honor the light of God.

Sometimes, when I'm sitting in the subway, I look at the people sitting all around me. They are all strangers and, very often, because I live in New York, they are from cultures different from mine. I see women reading Chinese newspapers, listen to men discussing politics in Farsi, and watch Hispanic girls compare makeup on their way to school.

I look at these people and I try to see past what is unfamiliar to me. I always notice bright shining eyes and laughter and smiles. I notice the friendships between people of so many different cultures. And how polite everyone is.

When you're looking for the divine light in people, you notice how that light is shared throughout the world. And it makes the light inside you a little bit warmer.

I really can't recommend it highly enough.

ט

Teth

Teth is the initial letter of the word *tov*, which means "good." The form of the teth is "inverted," thus symbolizing hidden, inverted good. Kabbalah scholars interpret this to mean that good is often unseen; we must search for it and uncover it.

Good is also one of the eight synonyms for "beauty" in Hebrew. *Tov* refers to the most inner, inverted, and "modest" state of beauty. At the beginning of Creation, the appearance of light is termed "good" in God's eyes: "And God saw the light was good."

Number: Nine

Biblical References: Nine levels of peace. Nine *sefirot* pouring blessing into *Malchut*. The numerical symbol of truth and eternity. Nine blessings of *Musaf* on Rosh Hashanah. Nine blasts of the shofar.

Torah Quote: "She saw that it was good."

TETH MEDITATION
"She saw that it was good."

The above quote is actually a paraphrase of what Moses' mother saw when she gave birth to him. And, it is also what God said when He first saw the world He had created.

Funny, isn't it? That a mother could look at her child and God could look at the world and have the same reaction.

This is precisely what Kabbalah asks us to do—notice similarities and connections and consider them.

Of course, as a mother, it doesn't surprise me at all that 1) a mother would look at her child and see the world in him and 2) that there is this echo in the Torah, because obviously God wants us to know that the world is in our children and that He connects with us as a mother connects with her child.

It's a thought that reassures me on so many levels. I hope it reassures you.

ׇי

Yod

Yod is the symbol for hand and is considered the opposite of aleph. Where aleph is spirit, yod is our spirit in the real world. It exists in time and in space. It isn't corporeal or illusory.

Yod is a small letter and it symbolizes, too, the light of God. God's light is both a contraction and, at the same time, the opportunity to expound on that contraction and create a new world. We are the result of that emanation and then we make the world brighter and lighter.

Yod is small, but it is full of possibilities.

Number: Ten

Biblical References: Ten divine utterances through which the world was created. Ten things created on the first day. Ten things created at dusk at the end of the first Friday. Ten generations from Adam to Noah and from Noah to Abraham. Ten kings ruled the whole world. Ten nations given to Abraham. Ten pure animals. Ten categories of forbidden magic. Ten battles of Joshua. Ten essential limbs of the body. Ten categories of the souls of Israel. Ten trials of Abraham. A minyan of ten men. Ten Commandments. Ten plagues. Yom Kippur—the tenth day. The Divine Name ten times on Yom Kippur.

Torah Quote: "The tenth shall be holy."

The number ten is perhaps the most repeated number in the Bible and it is, obviously, an important number in our secular life, as we base most of our numbering systems on ten.

YOD MEDITATION
"I can follow the light or turn away from it."

Does everything have a meaning or are some things random and coincidental?

According to Kabbalah, nothing occurs by chance and nothing is random. Because God is omnipotent, He knows and sees and orchestrates everything.

So, does this mean we have no free will? Well, this is a tough one. According to Torah and its commentary, we have free will, but we are given direction as to which choice will bring us closer to God and which will take us further away. God offers us these choices and we have the option to go in either direction. That is free will.

כ

Kaph

God must create the world continuously; otherwise Creation would instantaneously vanish. His potential is therefore actualized at each moment. This concept is referred to as "the power to actualize potential ever-present within the actualized." The literal meaning of the letter kaph is "palm," the place in the body where potential is actualized. This awareness is reflected in the custom of placing one palm on the other upon awakening, before reciting the *Modeh Ani* prayer.

Placing palm on palm is an act and sign of subjugation, similar to the act of bowing before a king. Kaph is also the root of the word *kipah*, the yarmulke or skullcap. In reference to the creation of man it is said: "You have placed Your Palm [kaph] over me." Adam, the first man, was called "kaph," as he was the head of our creation (not as in a hierarchy, but as in the beginning and the top).

Number: Twenty

Biblical References: Twenty pieces of silver, for which Joseph's brothers sold him. Twenty cubits, the maximum height of a sukkah. The twenty years Jacob worked for Laban.

Torah Quote: "I thank You, living and eternal King, for You have mercifully restored my soul within me; Your faithfulness is great."

KAPH MEDITATION
"Every day is a new day."

God gives us chance after chance to get it right. You may have heard the expression, "The definition of *crazy* is doing something over and over and expecting a different outcome each time." It took me a while to understand this idea, because I felt, for many years, that I had to behave in certain ways. The outcome of my behavior was often surprising to me. I thought my behavior somehow had little to do with the circumstances in which I found myself.

Of course, now I understand what that saying means, and I understand that God is always offering me opportunities to grow closer to Him. I don't always live up to this gift; I can be as immature and needy and whiny as the most stubborn two-year-old, but the important thing—and the difference between a two-year-old and me—is that now I know there is a better option. An option that will not only work on this plane (where people will respond more positively to my behavior) but on a spiritual plane, too.

When I find it in myself to remain calm, to consider others, and to focus on the Divine, then God will shine His light within me and around me.

ל

Lamed

The form of the lamed represents the aspiration of the truly
devoted pupil to learn from the mouth of the teacher. The literal
meaning of the letter lamed is "to learn" or "to teach." The seed
of wisdom, alluded to by the letter yod, descends from the brain
(Adam) to impregnate the full consciousness of the heart (Eve).
The heart aspires (upwardly) to receive this point of insight from
the brain. Lamed is the heart ascending in aspiration to conceive
and comprehend ("understand knowledge") the point of wisdom,
the yod situated at the top of the letter lamed.

Number: Thirty

Biblical References: Thirty days of the month. *Malchut* is acquired
through thirty attributes. Thirty generations from Abraham to the
destruction of the First Temple.

Torah Quote: "A tower soaring in air."

LAMED MEDITATION
"What we get isn't actually just given to us."

It's interesting that God asks us to learn more and know more in order to understand the world and His desire of us. Why doesn't He simply give us what we need so that we don't have to work?

I believe, and Kabbalah teachers say, that God has given each of us a collection of gifts and a purpose. To create a world that is reflective of Him, we must live divinely and that, in turn, will not be work, but will instead be joyful and pleasant.

Psychologists call this feeling "flow." It describes the timeless quality of our state of mind when we are completely absorbed in our work. And isn't that, in a sense, a connection to God? A state when we aren't self-conscious, but instead completely connected to something larger than ourselves. We aren't self-involved in those moments; we are open and free.

This state is what Kabbalah teachers believe we will reach when we read Torah as they do—freely and meditatively and joyfully.

Mem

Mem, the letter of "water" (*mayim*), symbolizes the fountain of the divine wisdom of Torah. Just as the waters of a physical fountain (spring) ascend from an unknown subterranean source (the secret of the abyss in the account of Creation) to reveal themselves on Earth, so does the fountain of wisdom express the power of flow from a superconscious source. In the terminology of Kabbalah, this flow is from *Keter* ("crown") to *Chochmah* ("wisdom"). The stream is symbolized in Proverbs as "the flowing stream, the source of wisdom."

Number: Forty

Biblical References: Forty days of the flood. Forty years of wandering in the desert.

Torah Quote: "Waters that have no end."

MEM MEDITATION
"Nature gives me a clue to the secret."

Here on earth, the vastness of the universe is reflected in the endlessness of the ocean. I believe that when we are sad or stressed one of the best things we can do for ourselves is look out into the sky or sea. The open space offers us an immediate serenity and peace of mind.

It's ironic, though, isn't it? On first consideration, we might think that the vastness of the world would be frightening—it's a reminder of our own smallness. But, in fact, studies have shown that nature can help us feel better if we're depressed or anxious. I believe that this is because we feel a connection to the universe and to God that cannot be explained, but only experienced. We are reassured in the face of the vastness of the world because we know we are an essential part of the only thing that truly matters—God's plan and creation.

נ

Nun

In Aramaic, nun means "fish." Mem, the waters of the sea, is the natural medium for nun, fish. The nun "swims" in the mem, covered by the waters of the "hidden world." Creatures of the "hidden world" lack self-consciousness. Unlike fish, land animals, revealed on the face of Earth, possess self-consciousness.

Number: Fifty
Biblical References: Fifty queries into the nature of Creation that God posed to Job. Fifty references to the Exodus in Torah.
Torah Quote: "For the earth will be filled with the knowledge of God, like waters cover the sea."

NUN MEDITATION
"Learn something new."

Orthodox Jews believe the Moschiach will come when all of us have done all we can to learn as much as possible. This is only one reason why education is so important to Jews. We believe that learning—both the act and the accomplishment—brings us closer to God in this life and, ultimately, will bring Him back to us in the next life.

Learning does not have to mean endless study or reading of Torah. The Ba'al Shem Tov was the first to teach that learning can be a spiritual knowledge that brings you close to God. But I believe, too, that someone who knows as much about the people they love, about cultures, about their trade and their interest, is also doing God a service. They are invested in the meaning of life and acknowledging the value of the gifts God gives us.

Samekh

The circular form of the samekh symbolizes the fundamental truth reflected at all levels of Torah and reality: The realization and awareness of inherent unity between beginning and end, "the endless cycle," a manifestation of God's transcendent light.

Number: Sixty

Biblical References: Sixty guards of King Solomon. Sixty queens in the Song of Songs. Sixty tractates of the Oral Torah.

Torah Quote: "Their end is enwedged in their beginning and their beginning in their end."

SAMEKH MEDITATION
"We are small in size, but big in spirit."

The day I was writing this section, I was listening to a radio show in which a well-known author was discussing the universe and its infiniteness. He said, "Don't we all wonder what would happen if we could peer out to the end of the universe?" If we did that, he said, we would only find ourselves "turned back into where we are. It's an endless circle."

This is it. Kabbalah and its understanding of the universe actually mirror the theory that physicists have come up with. It's a miracle of both spirituality and science; Kabbalah says that the big bang is true because God made it so.

Our end is our beginning and our beginning is our end.

ע

Ayin

Ayin relates to the word "eye," as in the "eye" of God. People often think that the eye of God watches them in judgment and they live in fear of that judgment. But, if you feel instead that you are living in concert with God—that you are doing his will and striving to do the right thing—then the eye of God is watching you in protection and love.

This idea reminds me of how much children love to be watched. It is, of course, the essence of knowing you exist—another person has his or her eye on you and watches you. Knowing that God has his eye on you is a way of knowing that you exist in the presence of another's life and that you matter.

Number: Seventy

Biblical References: Seventy Jewish souls that descended to Egypt. Seventy elders chosen by Moses; seventy sages of the Sanhedrin. Seventy years of King David. Seventy names of God; seventy faces of Torah. Seventy words of the Kiddush.

Torah Quote: "She became his wife and he loved her."

AYIN MEDITATION

"Even when it seems we have no choice, we always have the choice to love."

According to Kabbalah, the story of Jacob and Leah and Rachel is about choice. Jacob wants Rachel but is given Leah. He doesn't run away. Instead, he chooses to love Leah, as well as Rachel, and then ultimately, he is husband to them both.

Ignoring, right now, how odd this sounds to us today, Kabbalah teaches us that we can love someone, but we still do not know exactly who we are going to wake up with in the morning. We do not know what life has in store for us and our mate. We can be angry that the person we love isn't perfect, but we choose to love anyway.

Love is always a choice. Even if, for whatever reason, the person you love is impossible to live with, or if, perhaps, he or she chooses not to be with you, you can still offer that person, in your heart and soul, love.

Offering love, no matter what the circumstance, honors the other person, honors you, and honors God.

Pe

The mouth, the letter pe, follows the eye, the letter ayin, and is associated with the oral Torah, as opposed to the written word.

Much of what we learn in life is from what others say to us. In fact, while many of us covet and adore the written word (especially a writer, like me), what we remember is what people say. When we think of our teachers we remember people standing in front of a classroom, talking.

The oral word is important, because, as it is first written in Genesis, "God said, 'let there be light.'" He didn't write it down. Once we speak, our feelings and our thoughts are real and they exist. The word, which comes from our mouth, is all-important in the eyes of God.

This is why it is so important to speak well of others and to only use loving speech.

Number: Eighty

Biblical Reference: The age of Moses at the Exodus.

Torah Quote: "You are my witnesses," says God; "God's testimony is within you."

PE MEDITATION

"Show by example, not preaching."

Jews do not proselytize. We do not stand on corners or knock on doors or try to convert people. In fact, Jews do just the opposite: When people ask about becoming a Jew, we are supposed to wait until they ask us three times before we take them seriously. We want to make sure they are making this choice with full awareness.

How we live our lives, how we treat people, how we spend our time is our testimony to Jewish life. We do not have to tell people what it means to be a Jew; we have to show them with our example, just as we teach our children by setting an example.

We honor God by living a righteous life, and He offers us His blessing when we do so.

צ

Tzadik

The letter *tzadik* begins the word *tzelem*, which is the divine image of God, the one in which God created man. People of all religions believe that man was created in the image of God, but what does that mean? Does that mean we look like God? No, because God is not of form or matter.

We cannot become God and we can never know God fully—at least in this lifetime—but we can embody what God has (or at least what we imagine him to have), which is loving-kindness, goodness, generosity, and a creative spirit.

Living with the belief that you are of God's spirit, rather than a person who is simply God's creation, gives you a responsibility to offer other people what God has given you (and them). And then, when you meet someone who isn't living with God (or in his image) you can know how black their heart must feel without the light or spirit within them.

This generosity of spirit is what we receive in God's image.

Number: Ninety

Biblical Reference: The age of Sarah at the birth of Isaac.

Torah Quote: "Open for me an opening of repentance the size of an end of a needle, and I will open for you openings big enough for cattle and wagons to enter."

TZADIK MEDITATION
"Miracles happen."

There are so many miracles in the Torah: women giving birth to children at ages that are extraordinary to us, waters parting, bushes burning. Is it all true, or is it metaphor? Orthodox Jews believe the Torah is the word of God and, more than that, is the truth, while Reform Jews believe human beings wrote these stories in tribute to God.

Whatever your belief in this area, you can still recognize the reality of miracles. Children who survive accidents and adults who survive sickness are miracles. I believe that in this day and age two people who manage to build a happy, healthy family that lasts a lifetime create a miracle.

Miracles happen when we put our spiritual energy in the right place. When we do so, God steps in with His energy and transforms what we've done with a gift—usually a surprise. I think it's impossible to plan for miracles, but when they occur we are reassured that there is a divine presence. We can feel an appreciation not only for what has been given to us, but also for what we've done to bring about this new energy that has come into our lives.

ק
Kuf

In general, kuf stands for *kedushah*, "holiness." God's ever-present transcendence is always with us and we exist in his holiness.

People who grasp organized religion, but don't grasp the divine spirit of God within themselves, think of holiness as a set of rules: a church or synagogue is a holy place, the Torah or Bible is holy, for example. But, the fact is, it is all holy. Everything is holy and we must treat it as such—with respect and love.

I can't help but think of the song Joan Osborne sang a few years ago: "What if God were one of us?" We are taught that the Moschiach isn't another God, but a person who could be anyone and that when the world—the entire world—is ready and treats people properly, then he will have the opportunity to return the world to its rightful state of holiness.

This is an amazing belief, because it puts the power in all of us to be redeemed and to look at every person as the potential of all goodness that God has offered to us.

Number: One hundred

Biblical Reference: One hundred daily blessings.

Torah Quote: "He is grasped in all worlds, yet no one grasps Him."

KUF MEDITATION

"We all have an idea of God,
but we cannot really conceive of Him."

The above quote may seem like an oxymoron—something that doesn't really make any sense—but it sounds true, doesn't it? It really is true: We all conceive of God, but the fact is, our human limitations mean we can understand only a small bit of what He really is and what He really has in store for us. We can't truly know the vastness of God, as much as we wish we could.

And that ignorance isn't a bad thing. In fact, our uncertainty and our questions give us another one of His gifts: faith. Faith keeps us going. Faith allows us to know what we don't know. It is a sign of wisdom to know what you don't know in order that you may learn more.

ר

Resh

The two letters that fill the letter *resh* are yod and shin, spelling *yeish*, which means "something." It is deliberately vague. This letter reminds me of one of my favorite cartoons. Two scientists—they look like physicists—are standing at a blackboard with a long, complicated equation on it. In between the two parts of the equation are the words: "And then a miracle occurs."

This, in turn, reminds me of the ceiling of the Sistine Chapel, the moment Michelangelo captures: God stretches out his finger to Adam's finger. They don't touch, there is a space—a nothingness—but, in fact, "something" occurs: Man is created.

I believe that "something" is a vague word that can mean a multitude of beautiful things if we embrace the miracle of what we don't know in that space. George Harrison sang of "something in the way she moves" because he couldn't understand (or put into words) what made him love Patti Boyd (the woman for whom he wrote the song). Instead, he was content to live with the wonder of it all, the unknowingness of it. We don't "know" what "something" is, but we know it IS and our faith in that something is all that matters.

Number: Two hundred
Biblical Reference: Two hundred lights shine out of the self.
Torah Quote: "The King and His people."

RESH MEDITATION
"We should not have to choose between our God and our state."

Often there is a struggle between a person's spiritual beliefs and his or her political affiliations. Jews were often persecuted because they wouldn't put a pharaoh or a king in front of their belief in God. There is no king other than God. This is not to say that God is in any way political. It is simply to say that there is no affiliation that is more important than a person's connection to God. Nothing takes precedence, not even a love of family (witness the story of Abraham and Isaac), over our relationship with God. He is our King.

Shin

One of the meanings of the word *shin* in Hebrew is *shinui*, "change," which, at first glance, seems ironic, as we are told: "I am God, I have not changed." This means that God's essence has never and will never change no matter what goes on in the world.

Many of us fear change. We rely on the facts of our lives to remain consistent so that we can feel safe and secure. But I believe this is short-sighted. I have moved a lot in my life and people always tell me how scary that would be for them. But, the thing is, I carry with me all that is important: a belief in the goodness of people and a faith that I will do the right thing so that, in turn, the right thing will happen in my life and, more importantly, a strength that if things do go wrong, I will know how to handle whatever comes up.

If we can remain true to all that never changes then we will feel safer with the reality of life: it is always changing.

Number: Three hundred

Biblical Reference: Three hundred years Israel worshiped idolatry in the days of the Judges.

Torah Quote: "I am God, I have not changed."

SHIN MEDITATION
"God is Infinite."

God does not transform Himself or try to trick us or pretend to be something He is not. He is and always has been and will be forever as He is.

That certainty is a concept that can give us a lot of strength and courage. When you truly have faith in God, you feel a safety that is like no other because your faith is in something that will never change. Ever. God is the only thing in this life (even beyond death and taxes) that you can be sure of.

Taw

The Zohar states: "The taw makes an impression on the Ancient of Days." "The Ancient of Days" refers to the sublime pleasure innate within the "crown" (will) of divine emanation. The letter taw (here referring to the "Kingdom of the Infinite One, Blessed be He") leaves its impression on the "Ancient of Days." The impression is the secret of simple faith in God's ultimate omnipresence, the Infinite present in the finite, for "there is none like unto Him" (the conclusion of the above quotation from the Zohar).

This faith passes in inheritance from generation to generation, from world to world, the *Malchut* ("kingdom") of the higher world linked to the *Keter* ("crown") of the lower world. The taw, the final letter of the aleph-beth, corresponds to *Malchut*, the final divine power, in the secret of "Your Kingdom is the Kingdom of all worlds." The impression of the taw is the secret of the power that links worlds—generations—together.

Number: Four hundred

Biblical Reference: Four hundred years of exile in Egypt.

Torah Quote: "Leave your land, your family, and your father's house to the land that I will show you."

TAW MEDITATION
"The journey is spiritual, not physical."

Most of us do not leave the world we know. We are born, we marry and have families in the country where we were born, and then we die. But Jews have traveled throughout the world, as have other exiles, of course, searching for a home.

God doesn't send Abraham on a strictly physical journey. He sends him, too, on a spiritual journey—one that lasts his entire life.

And our spiritual journey also lasts our entire lifetime (and beyond).

CHAPTER FOUR

The Calendar

Because Kabbalah concerns itself with numbers and dates, the months of the year are of course quite important to Kabbalists. The Jewish calendar is lunar and so the dates don't directly correspond to the Juno calendar that Westerners use. However, the Bible does not advocate a belief in astrology (nor does it mention all the planets, which is what astrology is concerned with), and, according to biblical traditions, you should never make predictions (because God is at work in the future). Nevertheless, certain times of year are designated for certain types of spiritual studies. These interpretations are not based on astrology, but rather on the direct experience of living in certain seasons and on the seasonal relationship to biblical occurrences. (This is just one reason you should question any writer's discussion of the correlation between astrology and Kabbalah.) Jewish rabbis never, at any time, contemplate the deeper significance of being a Virgo or of someone's rising sign. There are, no doubt, Jewish astrologers, but they have little to do with biblical or Kabbalastic writings.

According to Kabbalah, each month has a permutation of the tetragrammaton (see Chapter Three), as well as Torah readings that go along with it. These Torah readings have inspired the suggested meditations I've given you. I've also offered a few general ideas of what time of year each month approximates according to the Western calendar.

One more thing. It's hard to say when a Jewish year actually begins. The first month of the Jewish year is Nisan, in the spring, and yet the New Year begins with Tishri, in autumn, after Rosh Hashanah. I've just chosen to go with Tishri, since that's when the Jewish calendar starts a new year.

Think of a year as a time period that will bring you closer to God.

We all set goals, whether they are short term (get up early tomorrow morning) or long term (in five years, I hope to own my own home). Kabbalah offers the idea that God has given us a year (a cycle, not a time limit) to be at one with the season and grow accordingly—just as trees and flowers do.

If you look at the year—and, as I mentioned, for our purposes we begin the year with Rosh Hashanah, the Jewish New Year that begins typically in late September/early October—you can see that it goes from birth to rebirth. In fact, someone once referred to it as the original twelve-step program.

The Jewish calendar provides a "self-improvement" intention for each month, as well as meditations and suggestions on how to live in harmony with the season.

Think of holidays not as celebrations, but as a time to reflect.

I am a Scrooge. I can say this with all honesty: I hate the holidays. I hate what they have become—a time to give gifts that put us into debt. A time to force yourself to be happy even though the weather is usually awful and you have to sit in traffic. And, I hate all the gifts I get. I am always reminded, each and every holiday, as I open up box after box of presents, how little my family knows me.

Of course, I don't like being this way. My attitude doesn't help anyone and it's just ugly, unattractive, and ungrateful.

So, here's what works for me: I sit with myself and think about what it means to have a family. To be so fortunate that I am surrounded by people with whom I have a common history. I think about the long history of each of these holidays and how I am part of a long, long story that began thousands and thousands of years ago.

Just changing my frame of mind changes not only my own experience, it also changes the experience of those around me: they don't have to deal with a Scrooge anymore!

(And yes, I know, it's ironic to use a Christmas symbol in a Kabbalah book, but my feeling is, if it works, use it.)

Get in touch with the moon.

The calendar Westerners live by is as made up as a calendar can be. It starts in the middle of the year, as far as I'm concerned. Whenever January 1 rolls around I always think, gee, this doesn't feel like anything. It has nothing to do with any of the holidays, it has nothing to do with winter, and it has nothing to do with how we feel during that time of year.

But the moon, the moon! I've never been one of those people who believes the full moon makes us crazy or anything, but I do believe that the moon is a wonderful thing to be in touch with. When it's new, we can start projects, set goals, make small changes. When it's full, we can celebrate our energy and our connection to life. And then, as it wanes, we can relax a little.

Each Jewish month begins with a new moon. In fact, the Hebrew word for month is *chodesh*, which means "newness." Now, it's not as if every month is exactly the same. We begin each month with a new goal and a new intention.

It's just amazing to me how God thought of everything—how it all works. How every day is a new beginning.

Tishri

The Jewish year begins with more holidays than any other month. Tishri includes Rosh Hashanah, Yom Kippur, and Sukkoth. On Rosh Hashanah, the Jewish New Year, we dip an apple in honey and eat it to symbolize our hopes for a sweet year.

Because of the holidays, we pray more during this month than during any other month. The Sages say that in this month the universe was created, which God did through the act of divine speech.

Tishri is Kabbalistically related through the word and letter lamed, which means "to learn." Why is learning the focus of the month? Because we must learn before we do. The beginning of the year is the time to remind ourselves that all beginnings must come from a place of wisdom and knowledge.

The first Torah portion of the year is the story of Adam and Eve in the Garden of Eden. In that garden were two trees, the Tree of Knowledge of Good and Evil and the Tree of Life, which, ironically enough, the Torah is often called. Adam and Eve were cautioned not to eat from the Tree of Knowledge of Good and Evil, yet they were allowed to eat from the Tree of Life.

Adam and Eve's mistake was eating fruit from the Tree of Knowledge of Good and Evil, which symbolizes experience, before eating from the Tree of Life, i.e., learning Torah. If they had first eaten from the Tree of Life, God would have then allowed them to eat from the Tree of Knowledge of Good and Evil. The lesson is that learning must come before doing.

For example, learning the principles of honesty starts a business off on holy ground. Learning about love helps a marriage get off to a good start. Learning principles of spirituality infuses our lives with meaning.

We should start the year off with as much Torah study as possible. We should strengthen our commitment to study in general.

And we should take this concept as a reminder to consult the wisdom of our heritage before beginning any new projects this year.

One of the reasons why Tishri is chock full of holidays and their mitzvoth is to help us begin a new year with a jump-start of merits. The custom is to take a spiritual accounting before Rosh Hashanah, the first day of Tishri. On Rosh Hashanah we are judged for the previous year. After Rosh Hashanah we start another year of accountability. God stacks the deck in our favor by starting off the year with a large number of opportunities for spiritual growth. The mitzvoth of shofar, fasting on Yom Kippur, and Sukkoth are all powerful ways to connect to God and our spirituality.

Justice and judgment are the heavenly influence for this time period. But by declaring God our King on Rosh Hashanah and showing Him we want to be close to Him throughout the holidays, we thereby mitigate the judgment and arouse divine mercy. It's God's way of letting us know the world stands in judgment. We respond by trying to come closer to Him.

The High Holidays of Rosh Hashanah and Yom Kippur are called the "Days of Awe" because they increase our awe of God. This is the connection to study and acquiring wisdom, as it says in Psalm 111: "The beginning of wisdom is the awe of God." Tishri, being the first month of the year, starts off a new annual cycle of acquiring wisdom by giving us an opportunity to gain more awe of our Creator. Tishri is a time of beginnings.

TISHRI MEDITATION
"Celebrate beginnings."

Hello. My name is Shoshanna and I am a "new beginnings" addict. Tomorrow, I always say, I will live better: eat healthfully, yell at my son less, enjoy what I have more. And, every day, I ask myself to be a little better and do a little more.

Beginnings are a gift, whether it's a new year or a new day, because we are blessed with opportunities and chances.

With new beginnings come responsibilities: not to squander the opportunities, but more than that, to make sure we follow through on what we've been given so that our next beginning doesn't involve doing something over but instead learning something new.

Think about next year, not this year. Where do you want to be, what new thing do you want to be doing? What do you have to do to get there? With those ideas in mind, you will be able to see what this day's new beginning should be.

TISHRI MEDITATION
"Value sex as a gift, not a recreation."

Surprised to see sex mentioned in this book? Well, Tishri is all about new life, and life begins with sex.

God gave us the gift of sex and made it highly enjoyable so that we would procreate in a reflection of his ecstasy of Creation. I believe that our attitude towards sex has gone through a transformation over the years that can only bring us closer to God.

Sex is neither meant to be political nor is it meant to be meaningless. I don't mean to be glib, but I believe there is a reason so many people reach for God when they attain orgasm. It is in this unconscious ecstasy that they feel closest to Him even while they are also feeling so ecstatically close to another person.

The next time you make love, imagine that you are going to be close not only to your partner, but also to God. I'm not saying this to embarrass you, but to suggest that perhaps being close to God will make sex more meaningful and even more joyous than it has been in the past.

TISHRI MEDITATION
"Recognize your failings and ask for forgiveness."

Sometimes, when we look back over our lives, we see decisions we made or hear things we said in anger, and can't get over our past. To help us learn, God has given us wisdom and intelligence, but He also offers us *teshuvah*, which means "return." It is sometimes translated as "repentance," but today that word has negative connotations, and *teshuvah* is as much about forgiveness as it is about recognition and understanding.

Even when you have sinned or transgressed, you are still connected to God, therefore you can always find your way back, because you never really lost your place in His spirit to begin with. Once you forgive yourself, you can get back to the path on which you are meant to walk: the righteous path.

Heshvan

When God created the universe, He also created the illusion of a separation between Himself and our world, His creation. His intention in doing so was to be sure we would return to Him on our own, and that we would have the option of welcoming Him into the world that He gave us.

The Torah outlines many ways to bring God into the world: loving your fellow human beings and being honest are just two. When we do good things, the presence of God (*Malchut*) is with us. We can even offer a prayer: "I am about to do this act in order to unify God's presence with His Creation."

King David's kingdom and the flood of Noah happened during this month. These are both examples of what happens in our universe when we separate ourselves from God.

Separation and return go together, however. God gave us the chance after Noah to prove our love for Him. Heshvan allows us to repeat that each year.

HESHVAN MEDITATION
"Get the job done."

It's easy to set goals, but it's difficult to accomplish them. So many people think, "Oh, I want to lose ten pounds," or "I want to make more money," but they don't create a plan to get there.

In this month, we put our New Year's plan into action. That means setting small goals that add up to the larger goal and, more than anything, drawing up an action plan that will allow you, each day, to get the job done.

For example, if you want to become more active in your community, you will, perhaps, need to make phone calls to determine which local groups can use your services. Then, you'll need to coordinate your schedule. And, finally, you will need to be committed and consistent.

Then, by the next New Year, you will have become more active in your community. If you don't create an action plan, though, then when Rosh Hashanah rolls around again, chances are you'll be setting the same goal. That's not good. Create a plan and your goals will be realized.

HESHVAN MEDITATION
"Fortify yourself."

This is the month of good eating. You might be surprised to find something so basic in a spiritual book, but food has always been an issue in the Torah—unleavened bread, not eating animals with cloven hoofs—God really cares about our diet!

If you struggle with your weight or your health, as so many of us do, remember that God wants to nourish you on both a spiritual and a physical level. He could have chosen not to give you a body—you could just be a divine light—but instead you are a light and a body, and you need to nourish them both equally well.

HESHVAN MEDITATION
"Be mindful of everyday routines."

Orthodox Jews say a blessing for just about everything they do in the day: waking up, eating, getting dressed, working, and sleeping. And now, more than three thousand years after the Torah was given to us, Oprah Winfrey has gone on national television suggesting that we all keep a gratitude journal, writing down a list of five things that we are grateful for every day.

It's easy to think of only the big things: a good job or excellent health or a wonderful spouse and children. But why not consider being thankful for the small things that make our lives so joyful and easy? Running water (or water in general), a breeze, the sunshine coming through the leaves on the tree, or the way children say funny things when they are first learning to communicate (just the other day, my son asked our neighbor for some "melonade," and she laughed so hard no sound came out). Isn't it these small moments that make our lives so sweet?

So, today, be mindful of the small moments and how they add up over time to make a joyous life.

Kislev

Often we think to ourselves, "If only I had beauty and money, then I would be okay. I could do the things I want to in life." The problem with this thinking is twofold. First, God gives us what we need to live our destiny. Second, when considering a goal, you can't think purely in practical terms. God gives us help when we put our faith in Him and our energy in the right direction.

This is the month of Hanukkah. A bit of oil that should have lasted only one day lasted eight instead, because God rewarded the energy of the Maccabees.

There is the story, too, of Akiva, a shepherd, who saw water dripping on a stone. He noticed a hole had worn through the stone where the drops were hitting it and said to himself, "If water can do this to a rock, imagine what the Torah can do to my heart." So he went off to study for many years, carrying with him the image of how much a little bit can add up to.

Do a little this month. It will add up to a lot.

KISLEV MEDITATION
"Light your darkness, illuminate your fear."

We often mistakenly believe that to be better people we need to ignore or overcome our fears.

I disagree.

I think that to grow we need to acknowledge and honor our fears. In fact, I think we need to let our fears sit next to us and exist while we go on to do the thing that scares us the most. If you are honest about your fear, you take away its power, and then you will have the energy to feel and honor your courage. And that will make you succeed.

So, tell people about your fear. Write it down. Be open and honest. Let it exist. In its existence its size and shape will become real and, oddly enough, less scary.

KISLEV MEDITATION
"Accept it: There is a light within you."

We fight it. We focus on our mistakes and shortcomings. We harass and berate ourselves. We judge ourselves unfairly. But, the fact is, God has put His light in you and it is. It exists, no matter what you are doing and whether or not you are paying attention.

It is important in this month simply to feel the light within you. The light that kept the Hanukkah candles glowing is the same light that will never go out in you, no matter what happens.

KISLEV MEDITATION
"Say thank you."

We all say thank you without thinking during the day: "Thank you for the coffee," "thank you for the change," "thank you for the memo." But why not say thank you for the things that matter? Thank a coworker for making your day brighter. Thank your family for sharing their lives with you. And, of course, thank yourself for what you do everyday to contribute to the peace and goodwill of the planet.

Tebet

In some religions the only people who go to Heaven are those who believe in that particular doctrine. Not Judaism. Jews believe that any righteous person can go to Heaven and that Jews who do not fulfill their potential will not get into Heaven.

Likewise, this month is characterized by perception—how we see things. It is not enough to be a Jew. We must lead a righteous life.

There is no good and bad or right or wrong. There is only intention.

TEBET MEDITATION
"Appreciate difficulties."

I have a friend who complains all the time. She actually once told me that life is too hard. "Really?" I said to her. "I can't believe how easy we have it. Everyone should have my problems."

I have problems, but I am grateful for them. I'm not trying to sound like I'm better than my friend, but I do feel that my attitude is more useful and, frankly, correct. Each problem I have is an opportunity to grow. Every issue I notice about myself—whether it's my tendency to be hard on people (and myself) or my tendency toward paranoia—is, I believe, a way that I can become a better person.

Growth is possible only when you notice areas that need tending. I have a pillow on my bed that says, "The courage to grow is noticed by the universe." In other words, by noticing a problem that you have and choosing to grow through it—to learn and become better—God will pay attention and good will come from directing your energy to the dark spots in your life.

TEBET MEDITATION

"Accept anger; process anger; let go of anger."

Anger is tough for a lot of us. Sometimes we hide from our feelings, which then makes us respond irrationally to situations that don't warrant real anger. And then, when someone does something that we legitimately have a right to be upset about, we suffocate our feelings.

Anger exists as legitimately as happiness does. The key to managing anger is to feel it, to be specific about those feelings, to communicate those feelings specifically, and then, to let it pass.

For example, when you are angry at your spouse, you can tell him what he did that bothered you, how it made you feel, and what you would like done about it. Now, you cannot bring up the past, you cannot make him responsible for your feelings, and, most important, you cannot expect that what you want done will be done. That's his option. He is not bound to make you happy. He is only bound to be respectful to you.

Then, after you have expressed yourself, you owe it to yourself and God to let the anger go and let the goodness back into your soul and connect with the generous light of God.

TEBET MEDITATION
"You have choice, but not control."

This meditation reminds me of the Serenity Prayer: "God, grant me the serenity to accept the things I cannot change, courage to change the things I can, and wisdom to know the difference."

It's important to understand that you have control over just one thing in life: yourself. You may be in charge of a lot (children, animals, a business) but all you ultimately control is yourself: your actions and your words. If you wake up every day knowing that all you can do is your very best and that the rest is up to God, then you will expend energy in the right parts of your life and not waste your time trying to control things that aren't up to you.

Giving up control is scary for some people, but once done, it is extraordinarily liberating. And, as the Serenity Prayer states, it is the wisest thing to do, which means God asks it of us in order to let Him do His job.

Shebat

We are commanded to "love God with all our strength, with all our hearts, and with all our might."

When I was little, I used to think this meant I should close my eyes really tightly and try—with all my heart—to love God fiercely. Now that I'm older, however, I know that God means this metaphorically. He means that, whatever I do, I should do it with love of God. If I eat dinner, I should do so in such a way that serves my love of God—by saying thanks, by appreciating what I have, by being mindful to the meal and to the people I share it with. If I do a task, I should be aware of its deeper significance—everything I do is an offering to God.

This idea is very Buddhist-y (one of my favorite words). It harkens to the idea of mindfulness. Buddhists recommend that you still the voices in your head with meditation so that you can be mindful (aware) of life around you as it happens. You detach from desire (wanting more and doing more) in order to simply exist in the present moment.

Jews, of course, place their faith in God as a Creator, so being mindful means more than simply being aware. It also means being conscious of your connection to the Creator.

Shebat is a month to focus on the idea of using your routine daily behavior as a medium for spirituality. This month, think through your work, play, exercise, eating, reading, and more, and focus on the spiritual side of these activities.

SHEBAT MEDITATION
"Do something new."

Being asked to be grateful for the big and small gifts in our lives means we sometimes pay so much attention to how we do things that we don't notice how we feel (aside from our gratitude). Our prayers can become as routine as any of our other habits: washing, eating, and sleeping.

God asks us to grow in this life, and growth demands taking risks and being challenged. Kabbalah reminds us to spice up our lives so we can taste the variety that God offers us. Whether it's a different way of cooking, a new route to work, or a conversation with a new person, don't become so wrapped up in your closeness with God that you forget to be part of the world you live in—the world God has given you.

SHEBAT MEDITATION
"Nurture yourself."

It is easy, during this time of year, to eat too much and to eat large amounts of unhealthy foods that are readily available, because we forget that winter will end and that, in a few months, we will be outside in the sunshine, enjoying the world around us. I am not talking about bikini weather. I'm talking about the Jewish calendar, which states that the sap of your energy is flowing right now; even if it feels static, you are still moving toward the goals that you set for yourself at Rosh Hashanah. Therefore, you need to take care of yourself with the knowledge and faith that this nurturing will pay off soon.

SHEBAT MEDITATION
"Know that just because you can't see it, doesn't mean it's not happening."

This meditation is related to trees, because in this month we are commanded to remember that sap is beginning to flow in the trees, even though we have no proof of it.

As I wrote this book, winter was turning to spring—and yet it was a very long winter. In fact, where I live, it felt like spring didn't begin until May, about two months after it officially begins.

Every night that year, when I read my son a story before he went to bed, we would look out the window at the bare maple tree in the backyard. I would always think to myself, "It seems like this year the leaves will never come."

But they did. Everything worked just as it was supposed to even though I was full of doubt.

Life is going on. We don't have to control it or do anything. In fact, rather than trusting that life goes on, we can simply rely on it. With that security, we are free to pray, to say thank you, and to do our work.

Adar

I am always intrigued by the words "anonymous donor" when I see them in programs at the ballet or in conjunction with social causes, such as in a donor list.

Of course, the benefits of being hidden should be taken in context. Sometimes things need to be revealed, sometimes things need to be hidden. There's a time and a place for everything. We have two Torahs, one revealed, one hidden: the Written Torah—the Five Books of Moses, the Prophets, and the Writings—is revealed, and the Oral Torah, which was handed down orally from teacher to student, is hidden. On a deeper level, the world of Kabbalah is considered the hidden wisdom and all other Torah knowledge is considered revealed. Now is the time to speak about hiddenness, because that is the essence of Adar.

Purim, the holiday in the middle of Adar, is all about things that are hidden. It is the story of Esther, whose name means "hidden," and the story shows the hidden hand of God in those events. On Purim, people wear masks to hide their identity and drink wine (lots of it) to reveal their hidden selves. In fact, drunkenness is mandatory on Purim.

Our souls are hidden so much of the time. Jews believe the soul is the divine spark—the light that connects us to God. This month, get in touch with your hidden self.

Your hidden self is a joyful self, according to the Rabbis. The Talmud says, "When Adar begins we increase our joy." This month we infuse our divine spark with happiness. True happiness comes from using the pleasures of this world to elevate our consciousness and bind our thoughts to spirituality. That is the opportunity of this month.

Now is the time to reveal the joy hidden inside you. Now is the time to uncover the love you have for people and for God's world. If we each do these things just a little, imagine how happy and joyful the world would be.

ADAR MEDITATION
"Get drunk."

Surprised to see this advice in a book on spirituality? Well, Purim, the holiday we celebrate at this time of year, is all about drunkenness. Rabbis get drunk; men and women get drunk. And while children certainly don't drink, they do all they can to be happy (of course, fortunately, they don't have to work at it like we adults do).

Why do we drink? Because we do not want to feel any separation between ourselves and the ecstatic happiness of God. Personally, not being much of a drinker, I can testify to how close I feel to God when I am dancing to rock and roll music—that lack of self-consciousness combined with the way the music takes me out of my head brings me closer to God than anything else.

This joyfulness and this ecstatic meditative quality is what Kabbalah offers its students, because it takes you out of your conscious head and into your receptive, happy body and soul.

If you can't drink, or if you choose not to, lose yourself another way, such as through dancing, meditative walking, or singing. Anything that brings your focus out of your head and into a feeling of overwhelming closeness to the universe will work.

ADAR MEDITATION
"Be joyful."

I am sometimes overwhelmed by the sadness and cruelty in this world. I can become particularly upset by child abuse and wonder how I can be happy in a society that has so much violence. I try, in these moments, to remember that someone who is overwhelmed by pain can accomplish very little. Instead, I truly believe that feeling warmth and joyfulness inside—God's love—is the only energy that can bring about positive change. I try to retain my joyfulness not to be happy in a foolish way, but to offer gentle love to everyone I meet. I believe that the more serenity I have within me, the more able I am to be a force for positive change in the world.

The story of Esther—which we celebrate this month during the holiday of Purim—is a good example of this. Although Esther was angry at what Haman was planning for the Jews, she offered love and affection to her husband in order to bring more peace into the world. And it worked. She saved the Jews.

ADAR MEDITATION
"Let go of what doesn't work."

Many years ago I had a job that I struggled with. Not because I couldn't do the actual tasks, but because I had a lot going on in my life and I couldn't really find the energy to do my job as well as I needed to. Plus, I brought my home life to work.

One day my boss told me that I couldn't go on the way I was. If I didn't change my attitude, I would most likely lose my job.

Now, I want to say, there were real issues in my life at that point: someone close to me had died and I was getting divorced. Things were tough. But after my boss said that to me, I went home and made a conscious decision to change. And I did. A few months later I got a raise and a promotion.

My boss did me a bigger favor. She taught me a lesson. I think of that time now and I pay attention to whether or not things are working in my life. And if they are not working, I change. I let go of what doesn't work. I don't hold on to things out of fear. Instead, I grow, and that growth, as I mentioned earlier, is noticed by the universe.

Nisan

This month is all about *Pesach*, or Passover, a holiday that tells the story of the Jews' escape from Egypt. Children adore Passover because we read a story and do little bits of things as the story goes along—drink salt water as bitter as our tears, eat horseradish, break the matzo. It's a wonderful celebration.

I use a Haggadah (the book Jews read from on Passover) that honors not only the Jews who escaped Egypt thousands of years ago, but also the numerous Jews who, over the years, have escaped atrocities during our own time. Jews who fled pogroms in Russia and Jews who fought back against the Nazis in Germany are in my Haggadah.

What I remember most about Passover as a child was having my aunt and uncle, who are Auschwitz survivors, listen to these stories. My aunt and uncle, not surprisingly, had a terrible time during World War II. Born and raised in Poland, they managed to elude the Nazis by being part of a resistance group that hid in the woods for two years. They were captured eventually and sent to Auschwitz. Decades after those childhood Passovers, I met them in Brooklyn. My uncle had maintained his religious beliefs but my aunt had no use for God anymore; she never got over what happened to her (as I told another relative, I'm not sure anyone is supposed to get over the awful things she lived through).

Nevertheless, having both of them in my life gave me much to consider. Is it worth it to be a Jew when the world hates you and conspires to annihilate you? Why not take the easy road and renounce Judaism? Why believe in God if He allows these terrible things to happen?

I believe, more than anything, that this month is about choice. You have the choice to be connected with God. You don't have to be. You can be born Jewish and ignore God forever. You can be born into any religion and ignore your divinity as well as the divinity around you.

This month we celebrate people who never gave up. They honored their beliefs and their holiness to keep their spirits alive. That is really what faith is all about.

NISAN MEDITATION
"Liberate yourself."

Life can become an endless routine of work, family, and housekeeping. So many of us do the same thing day after day and wonder why we feel exhausted. We need stimulation. Nisan, a springtime month, reminds us to break it up a little and liberate ourselves from routine and habit.

In doing so, we are free to connect with God, because we remove our inner selves from the outer world and connect to the universal truth and infiniteness that is Him.

NISAN MEDITATION
"Liberate someone else."

As I mentioned earlier, Jews do not proselytize, but it is possible to offer wisdom and guidance to someone, a friend or a stranger, without mentioning your religion. If someone comes to you with a struggle or a concern, you can suggest that, instead of worrying about the day to day, you have found that it is more worthwhile and peaceful to connect to God and the big picture instead.

Not everyone, of course, will understand what you are referring to. People are very caught up in the *mishigosh*—Yiddish for "drama." But you can try to liberate people from that drama by directing their attention to what is beautiful and good within them. Many people never learn this way of life from their family and friends, so it will seem foreign to them, but you will have offered them liberation and, over time, that peacefulness will shine its light within them in a larger way.

NISAN MEDITATION
"Tell a story."

For many Jews, Passover is a favorite holiday because, like our other holidays, it involves a great story—suffering, rescue, high drama, learning. Passover has it all (except romance). We are commanded to tell the story as part of our holiday celebration. This is a wonderful thing to do, and I believe that storytelling is the best teaching tool we have. This is why, as I'm sure you've noticed, I've told so many stories in this book. Stories, like the Torah itself, are an art form people like. Metaphor seems to say more than fact.

So, this month, tell someone, especially a child, a story. Tell someone about yourself or about a member of your family. Let the person know that the spirits of your ancestors live on in your stories. My grandmother, who was the second youngest of eleven children, told incredible stories of what it was like to grow up Jewish in Brooklyn at the turn of the last century. Those stories disappear if we don't continue to tell them. Telling them honors the past and our history, which is, to God, a mitzvah.

Iyar

There is a fifty-day period between Passover (last month) and Shavuot (next month) called the Omer period. Torah commands us to count the days between the two holidays. To count every day takes a certain commitment and discipline. Some people end up missing a day here and there. This daily counting is an indication of the spiritual potential of the month of Iyar.

There are seven weeks of counting, which are linked to the seven lower *sefirot* (see Chapter One: *Chesed, Gevurah, Tiferet, Netzach, Hod, Yesod,* and *Malchut)*. You "count" these days not numerically, but by making them mean something. To make something count, you should strive for wisdom and depth of meaning.

Pick a quality or an attribute for each day, such as happiness, kindness, or generosity, and focus on it for that day. If it's generosity, see how many ways you can be generous and notice how different it feels than the way in which you usually live your life. Make the month count.

IYAR MEDITATION
"Detox."

This month is a wonderful time to get rid of the sluggish energy we have accumulated during the winter. There are two ways to detox, or get rid of toxins in the body. One is physical—eat and drink only fresh food and water in small amounts. The other is spiritual—get rid of feelings and habits that bog you down and inhibit your inner light. Imagine, for a moment, the light inside you and ask yourself whether something is blocking it. Are there shadows? If so, seek to purify yourself through prayer and, as the Buddhists say, right thinking and right deeds—in other words, thinking and deeds that do no harm. Right thinking and right deeds will lighten your load and you will physically feel freer and purer.

IYAR MEDITATION
"Remember those who are gone."

When someone passes away, Jews mourn for a year and then are commanded to move on with their lives and be alive, as in not exist solely as someone who is bereaved. However, that certainly doesn't mean that we forget those we have loved. I believe we should all make it a point to remember those from our past in private and public ways. Privately, you can say a prayer for people who aren't with us anymore. Publicly, you can share your memories with friends and family—discuss the person you miss and say it out loud.

I am always amazed at how, when I tell someone, for example, that I miss my grandmother, the other person will often tell me about who he or she misses. In that moment I always feel a connection not only with the other person, but also with the eternal light to which we are all connected. Suddenly, four people, two living and two dead, are connected on a spiritual level. It's quite meaningful and takes us out of the everyday and into the realm of the eternal.

IYAR MEDITATION
"Connect with someone."

It is risky to tell someone how you feel. It is much easier to keep your mouth shut or, worse, outwardly agree to what someone says even when you don't inwardly feel the same. We feel that by agreeing with someone we will connect. But that is not true. In order to truly connect with someone else, we must be honest—about our feelings and our thoughts.

This doesn't always work, of course. Someone may disagree with you or perhaps your feelings won't be validated. Rather than look to connect with a thought or feeling inside yourself, offer a connection to someone else. When someone is telling you about his desires, listen to him with sincerity and repeat back what you heard. Let him know that you believe in him and that you offer support. In this way, you will make a connection because your intention is to do so. That is the only way the connection can be made—if it is your intention to connect.

Sivan

This is the month in which Jews received the Torah, the most important thing that has ever happened in our history. We have been given something—revelation—the story and reason for our existence.

The Torah is the most awesome gift that could be given, way out of proportion to any effort we could put in. The Zohar says that God and the Torah are one. It's not just wisdom, stories, and moral instruction; it's a piece of godliness in the physical realm. It's the "mind" of God, the "will" of God. It's the clearest expression and understanding of God we can have while alive. Thus, the word *Torah* is synonymous with *Yichud Hashem*, the oneness of God.

The most important aspect of being given Torah isn't that it was a gift; it was something we earned. Jews received Torah because they didn't idolize other gods, because they led lives of purity, and because they left places that didn't welcome them while still believing in God. In turn, God gave us Torah. We were still thankful, though. We still worked. We still continued on. We didn't say, "Thanks, now we're going to sit back and relax." We kept going.

This is the month when we are both rewarded and commanded to keep going. It's all, really, one and the same moment.

SIVAN MEDITATION
"Be open."

It is summertime, and the weather asks us to spend more time outdoors. Being outdoors invites us to stay out of our heads, doesn't it? Summer isn't the time for school, but for vacation. It isn't the time for work, but for fun. We may think, perhaps, that we cannot focus on our devotion to God.

This isn't true. We can be as devoted as ever when we are happy and having fun. Our connection to God is not based on seriousness; it is based on awareness and appreciation. Even if you are playing Frisbee on the beach—especially when you are playing Frisbee on the beach—you can be open to the feeling of closeness you have with the life God has given us. He gave us the beach and the Frisbee as well as the synagogue and the Torah, so there is no reason not to take your fun as seriously as you take your study.

Be open to the possibility that God dwells in everything and that prayer and devotion are possible in every situation.

Tammuz

Tammuz, according to Kabbalah, has a strong relationship with the realm of sight. It brings to mind a quote that takes us right to God: "Lift up your eyes to the heavens, and see who created these stars." If you look at the stars, you can see God's Creation and know Him. Even Einstein, a man who understood the universe in ways few of us can, said, "God doesn't play dice." In other words, God knows what He's doing.

It also says in Tanach, "A wise man has eyes in his head." I love quotes like this, because they seem as though they say nothing and everything all at the same time. Basically, this quote means, "Use what you have and pay attention." When you pay attention to what is around you and allow the information to come into your head and then process it properly, you will figure it all out and you will come to God with humility and acceptance of what He can do. You will strive to connect with Him through your heart and soul.

All because of the eyes in your head.

TAMMUZ MEDITATION
"If you feel separate, let it be."

This month, we are commanded to let difficult and unpleasant feelings exist. Many addiction problems, whether shopping or overeating or drinking or gambling, develop when we attempt to deny our feelings of inferiority and fear. To escape unpleasant realities, we turn to behaviors that have nothing to do with our real lives. But these behaviors soon take over our real lives and our real selves and we then have a new problem to deal with.

This month, sit with your feelings. If you feel alone in the world, or scared about your inability to do something, stay with the feeling. It will pass—that much I can promise—and once you've allowed it to exist, it will get smaller, and once it is smaller, it won't matter so much.

The first step toward change is allowing your feelings—even the scary ones—to exist. It is a challenge, but I can assure you that it is a challenge that will reward you in very big ways.

TAMMUZ MEDITATION
"If you feel quiet, be silent."

Oh, my goodness, one thing you can say about writers is that we love to talk! If we're not talking with our mouths, we are talking with our fingers. And while I don't deny the power and goodness of words, I am the first to celebrate the beauty and serenity of silence. It was almost an exercise for me to learn how to be silent. I grew up in a home where noise was a way of life—TVs, discussions, stereos—if it was noisy, it happened in my house. Today, as an adult, I live in a quiet home. Oh, we play music and we watch TV, but when we do those things, we do them consciously, not just as background noise. We talk when we need to and are silent when we don't. I can't tell you how truly liberating this is, and how much I feel my son gains from this. God commands us to speak and write, but He also commands us to rest and be silent.

TAMMUZ MEDITATION
"Accept what is."

I am a person who dwells in possibility and dreams. I often have to remind myself to keep my feet on the ground and to honor the tasks of daily living. That is why I appreciate reality-based people so much. People who manage their lives more efficiently than I do are almost miracle workers to me. It isn't that my daily life is out of control—I pay my bills and I do my job and take care of my son—but my head is often in the clouds. At the same time, I know people who do the things I do and keep their heads right where they belong.

Today, even as you connect to the divine light, consider noticing what is right in front of you. Meditation and prayer and closeness to God occur when we are aware of the life around us, not just aware of His presence. God asks us to be in the moment. By accepting the realities of daily life, we are better able to accept the realities of life—what we have control over and what we don't. The small picture can lead us to the big picture, rewarding us with an even deeper connection to God.

Ab

Traditionally, this is a sad time of year, because it is the month in which Jews lost the First Temple. It has been so long since we've had the First Temple that we've forgotten what we're missing. Many of us walk around feeling a loss, but we don't know what we're grieving for. We turn to drugs or superficial companionship or TV to fill the hole in our souls.

By awakening the recognition of what we need and want, we create a greater potential for God to bestow it upon us. We can look to Him to fill our hearts, and with His energy, we can connect to others and His Creation with a fullness of spirit.

I once had a friend who had lived through a lot of pain and tragedy. He fought in a war, and he lived the life of a firefighter. He bottled up his sadness and anger for years. Then he found a solution: a connection with God that worked for him. "I still feel my feelings," he said, "but it's cleaner."

Don't run away from your fear and sadness. Let them sit next to you. Then, look to God for the connection. He's always there.

AB MEDITATION
"Recognize that life is sad and beautiful."

"Life is sad and beautiful," said the Roberto Begnini character in the film *Life Is Beautiful*, and I have found it to be so. We expect life to be happy and fun. To be fair. We expect life to make sense. We are surprised when it doesn't and sometimes wonder why God has made it so.

I have come to believe that to expect life to be pretty would be to miss out on the full range of human experience—the ultimate gift of God. Don't we appreciate the people who seem to have lived a full life, rather than the people who seem to have it all? We admire people with rich experiences—a life that has a little salt and a little sugar.

AB MEDITATION
"Refrain from judgment."

I believe that I am on a journey to become closer to God, and I have friends and companions who are on that same journey. But not everyone in my life has this same goal. It is sometimes—actually, often—difficult for me not to judge these people. Their concerns are not my concerns. At the same time, they do not appreciate the way I live my life, and I feel that their values are not the same as mine.

Does that make me better than them? I have to admit that sometimes I think it does. When I get that way, I realize that I am not behaving in the way God wants me to. The people I am judging are on their own paths and, for all I know, are well on their way to bliss. I cannot say, because I do not know all.

I am reminded of the message, associated with some New Age spirituality: "There is more to come." In other words, just because you think you know what something looks like doesn't mean that you do.

Elul

The Hebrew calendar year ends with Elul, but when it comes to endings, it's important to remember: When a door closes, a window opens. Although we, hopefully, have reached some goals and learned more in the past year, we look forward to even more learning and growth in the year to come. A door is closing on the past, but the window to the future is open.

The Talmud teaches that Jews will reach their glory in Tishri, the next month (the first month of the New Year). Before then, however, it's only appropriate that those who will receive their glory understand the truth about themselves. During Elul we are asked to wake up from our metaphorical slumber and focus on growth.

ELUL MEDITATION

"Look at what you haven't done and love yourself anyway."

It's easy to feel guilty for what we didn't do this year. We still haven't lost weight; we still haven't accomplished a goal. Do not punish yourself with guilt. Real growth can come only through forgiveness. You did the best you could, and you will do better when you offer love and support to yourself. But don't worry; this doesn't mean you won't accomplish your goals. You will, because you have made a commitment to do so. But first, you must love and forgive yourself.

ELUL MEDITATION
"Get ready."

The end of the year is upon us and, as such, we must begin to wrap up the past. If you sense that you haven't done all you wanted to do in the past year, you have time to make amends. The time of judgment will soon be upon you—not only the time for God's judgment, but also the time for self-judgment. Therefore, be conscious of the time of year.

I'm never surprised that this is often when people bring a tough book to the beach rather than a romance novel. They think, "I should get around to reading *Moby Dick* by now." And they're right; they should. Whether it's reading a classic novel or starting an exercise program or increasing the amount of time you pray, now is the time to do it. By the end of the year, you will have developed a habit that will allow you to move forward into the new year.

Think Mitzvoth

To many Jews, the most meaningful story is about Rabbi Hillel, who converted a gentile by telling him, "That which is hateful to you, do not do to your neighbor. That is the whole Torah; the rest is commentary. Go and study it."

I love writing and I am grateful for my relationship with God. I am grateful, too, for the opportunity to write about what I've learned over the years. I hope you've enjoyed this book, but more than that, I hope it has inspired you to study and meditate on what matters. Thoughtfulness and mindfulness can only help bring about a genuine peacefulness in the world. This book is my mitzvah to you.

About the Author

Shoshanna Cohen grew up in a reform Jewish family who lived amidst the Orthodox Jews of Williamsburg, Brooklyn. This curiosity about a culture close to, but foreign to, her own, began a spiritual quest that sent her to school to pursue graduate studies in Eastern religion. After marrying and having children, Ms. Cohen became a Kabbalah student in New York City. This is her first book.

10-MINUTE CELTIC SPIRITUALITY
by Rosemary Roberts
ISBN: 1-931412-30-8
$12.00 (£7.99)
Paperback; 238 pages
Available wherever books are sold

EMBRACE THE CELTIC SPIRIT

This wonder-filled guide to the Celtic spirituality reveals the sacred secrets of the ancient Celts—from the magic of lore and legend to the divine mysteries of the saints.

With the help of hundreds of tips, meditations, and simple rituals, you'll master the intricacies of this time-honored tradition, and incorporate its blessings and benefits in your life.

Along the Celtic path you'll:

- Create new family traditions and celebrations for every season
- Bless your spirit with the grace of Celtic saints
- Draw upon the powers of the North, South, East, and West
- Incorporate nature's magical elements into your home and office
- Discover your unique totems and other symbols of strength
- Learn the age-old, esoteric language of the Druids
- Cast runes to determine your future

With *10-Minute Celtic Spirituality*, you'll bring the timeless inspiration, wisdom, and mysticism of the ancient Celts into your own life.